Book 2: Grades 6–8

Book 2: Grades 6–8

ROCKIN' ROOT WORDS

Manisha Shelley Kaura and S. R. Kaura, M.D.
Illustrated by Zak Hamby

First published in 2010 by Prufrock Press Inc.

Published in 2021 by Routledge
605 Third Avenue, New York, NY 10017
2 Park Square, Milton Park, Abingdon, Oxon OX14 4RN

Routledge is an imprint of the Taylor & Francis Group, an informa business

Copyright © 2010 by Taylor & Francis Group

Illustrations © Zak Hamby
Cover and Layout Design by Marjorie Parker
Illustrated by Zak Hamby

ISBN: 9781032143637(hbk)
ISBN: 9781593634155(pbk)

DOI: 10.4324/9781003237778

DEDICATION

To our respected parents and teachers, who make a difference.

ACKNOWLEDGEMENTS

We would love to assume all of the credit for this work; alas, this is not true. The work we have done, like any work, was built upon established knowledge. We owe debts of gratitude to Samuel Johnson, Noah Webster, the Oxford English Dictionary, Morrises, Robert Barnhart, and many other experts and researchers. We are also grateful for the countless teachers who work day and night to help children learn our marvelous mother tongue.

Many wonderful people have helped us—teachers, critics, and students. To name a few: Sheri Kozlowski, Cheryl King, our "gophers" Shawn and Sasha Kaura, Ms. Emily, Michaela Dew, and last and not least our volunteer project manager Monika Kaura (Manisha's Mom) who worked tirelessly to meet the deadline.

Several people were employed to move the manuscript from a chaos of word lists to a publishable product. Although they were paid for their service, we could never hope to pay them enough. We hope our heartfelt thanks will make up the difference. We want to thank Ms. Lacy Compton of Prufrock Press who made our life a lot easier by her skillful editing.

This daddy/daughter team put our heart and soul in the book you hold in your hands. We are grateful that you have picked it up and hope that you find it useful.

Very respectfully,
Manisha Shelley Kaura
S. R. Kaura

CONTENTS

Introduction   **ix**

Chapter 1: Numbers   **1**

Chapter 2: Quantifiers and Size   **23**

Chapter 3: Time   **39**

Chapter 4: Location, Directions, and Relationships   **51**

Chapter 5: Shapes, Qualities, Colors   **73**

Chapter 6: Bodily Structures   **89**

Chapter 7: Bodily Senses and Emotions   **105**

Chapter 8: Family, Home Life, and Religion   **127**

Chapter 9: Government and Society   **147**

Chapter 10: Roots of Motion   **165**

Answer Key   **186**

References   **193**

About the Authors   **195**

Common Core State Standards Alignment   **197**

INTRODUCTION

About This Book

We live in an age where we are totally bombarded by multimedia from all sides of our daily lives. Therefore, I wanted to create a tool that helped children learn while utilizing visual learning styles, so prevalent in our present day framework, namely our reliance on technology. The main purpose of the book series is to help children become better at managing information.

The largest part of this information comes to us in the form of the fundamental units of language which we refer to as "words." These words are not arbitrary solid blocks of letters put together but instead are made out of consistent word parts or chunks of letters. Here we will focus on the internal structure of the words, also known as "word parts" and "root words." The hope is to create independent word learners.

Although simple words like car are made out of small word parts, as taught in lower elementary schools, what we learn in higher education is that more complex academic words are made out of Greek and Latin word parts. A vast body of research has shown three compelling reasons for why every child should learn language using word parts. First, these word parts are scattered throughout our academic studies. Secondly, the human brain can easily capture word parts and retain them as patterns. Thirdly, after retention, patterns are stored systematically and permanently and can be recalled from memory for figuring out or decoding new words.

The seed for this book was planted when I was 9 years old, in the fourth grade. My Dad and I studied my sheet of vocabulary words sent home from school daily. While working on the homework, we talked more about actual words and would note that a large majority of the words appeared to have a consistent internal structure. We also noticed that some words had similar beginnings, endings, and guts. While researching the words more closely, we realized that the words did not just fall from the sky, but instead were constructed by someone who wanted the language to be more easily understood. Therefore, we further researched who, when, how, and why our language came to be.

As we pursued answers to all those questions, we studied dictionaries and etymology books; then Dad and I prepared multiple lists of the word parts and classified them into categories like prefixes, roots, and suffixes, and later divided them thematically into chapters. By making the lists, we wanted to construct a user-friendly manual in which our main goal was to introduce the complicated and esoteric field to children who do not possess significant knowledge of language study. The following paragraphs will elaborate further on the three compelling reasons mentioned before.

First of all, Greek and Latin word parts contribute to more than 60% of English, 70% to 90% of science terminology, 71% of social studies terminology, and a large part of mathematical terms (Farstrup & Samuels, 2008; Green, 1994). These roots are distinct and consistent to children learning the language. Students who learn Greek and Latin roots of the English language enjoy advantages such as comfort with big words, advanced awareness, and spelling improvement in science and technical language (Thompson, 2002). By studying these word parts, we will be able to understand the internal structure of words and learn word families, including those from other languages.

Secondly, the most compelling reason that we must learn using word parts is to see how scientifically the human brain functions as a pattern detector. We ultimately see patterns everywhere in nature, whether it is the wings of a butterfly, stripes on a zebra, or the color spectrum of a rainbow. In lower elementary grades this strategy has been used very successfully. When we analyze common words like car, it has an onset "c" and a rime "ar." Here you can use pattern "ar" and make words like tar, jar, bar, and so on. Another example pattern is "ook," used so one can learn words like cook, book, look, and took. Patterns like "ar" and "ook" are meaningless parts of a word, but nonetheless are very useful in building a large vocabulary in children.

As we move to upper elementary or middle school grades, we encounter words with Greek and Latin roots, prefixes, and suffixes. Let us analyze the word "exit," which has two word parts, "ex," which means out, and "it," which means to go. Therefore, we are able to recognize that an exit sign in a building tells you where to go out. The word atom is made from "a" which means no and "tom" which means cutting. The Greeks were brilliant, and without the help of an electron microscope, they still knew that if you kept on cutting any matter, then eventually you would not be able to cut it anymore and that smallest particle was labeled as an atom. Another example is reincarnation. Here logic is as useful as it is in math: re + in + carn + ation = again + into + body/flesh. When adding up the meanings to the word you can see that reincarnation means "a soul going back into the body or flesh again." You can probably see now that these are meaningful word parts that can be combined flexibly to make thousands of words. Therefore, learning the word parts is like a shortcut to mastering the English language. A benefit to such pattern learning is a higher level of comprehension with the context area text.

The third most compelling reason is the scientific-psycholinguistic process of storing and retrieving the words. We can input vocabulary in various ways. For example, if you learn one word at a time using rote memorization like denture (artificial teeth), dentist (tooth doctor), dental (pertaining to teeth), and dentine (part of a tooth), it will be stored in the brain separately lacking connections, just like free floating balloons as shown in Figure 1. Here words are free floating because they are not anchored at all. Suppose we tie these words together in a linear fashion using the root "dent" as the common feature (linking orthographically; see Figure 2). It will help children link the words together, and in return makes them easily retainable to memory. Still, this chain is only partially anchored in the brain. Later, more related words with the root "dent," like dentate, indentation, and indentured can be tied in and ultimately increase one's vocabulary.

Finally, we can take this process further by classifying these word parts thematically and memorizing them as concepts (see Figure 3). We can tie the words together in visual webs to increase learning because we know visual memory contributes 70% to 90% of learning in humans. Such a strategy can improve reading comprehension, vocabulary, spelling,

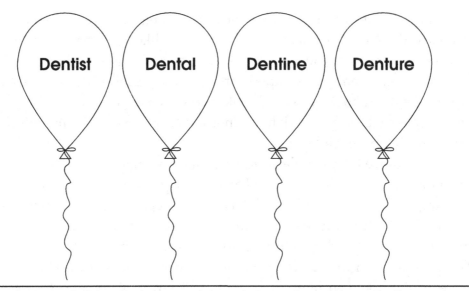

Figure 1. Individually learned words by rote memorization.

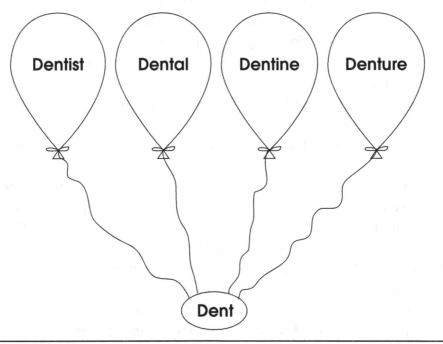

Figure 2. Orthographically-linked learned words.

and word building. The brain learns not in a linear fashion, but instead in a highly interrelated web fashion so that information can be retrieved quickly.

How to Use This Book

This book displays word parts in three ways:

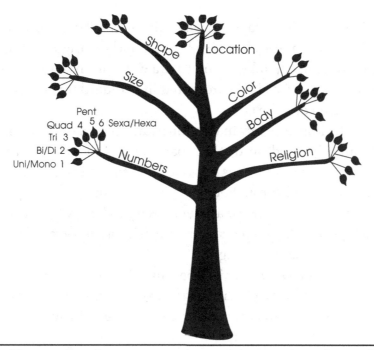

Figure 3. Thematically arranged as webs and root words learned as concepts.

- Word beginnings—Greek and Latin prefixes, roots, and some combining forms and loan words;
- Word endings—Greek, Latin, and English suffixes used to make nouns, adjectives, verbs, and adverbs; and
- Root words—arranged thematically with some loan words and some combining forms.

The book is divided into 10 overview chapters based on various themes within our language. Within each chapter are lessons containing 5–10 words for children to learn, each based on one or more topic areas. For example, within the numbers chapter, students will encounter a lesson on words related to one hundred and one thousand. Each of the lessons contains one or more word parts that define the lesson's content.

Each word part is presented in the following manner:

Sper comes from Latin, signifying hope or expectation.

Beginning	Root Word	Ending	New Word	Definition
de	**sper**	ate	desperate	dangerously reckless or violent, as from urgency

The new word part is given in italics, with an etymological note following it. This information is followed by at least one, but often many, instances in which the word part is used in the construction of an English word (or sometimes a word borrowed from another language!). The word is presented in exploded form, to draw attention to the word part in question, then the word is represented in standard form. Finally, a definition appears on the right.

Many of the lessons contain web illustrations to help show how one word part can help build words that span the language. For example, although "bio" means "life," it is not relegated to the life sciences. Several cartoons are scattered throughout the lessons to increase comprehension, and each lesson concludes with a brief activity to help students use their new knowledge. Finally, each chapter ends with a review activity to help children reinforce their learning.

We hope and believe that this program will impart a lasting understanding of the English language to all students, not just a familiarity with the words that we have the space to include.

CHAPTER I

Numbers

Numbering units can be as easy as the common 1, 2, 3, that we use every day or more complicated, such as the Roman numerals I, II, III. These numbers can even be represented with word prefixes, like uni-, di-, or tri- (which mean one, two, and three, respectively).

Numbers give a total count, amount, sum, or quantity. The word number comes from the Latin (through French)—*numerus*. We recognize a number as a digit, unit, quantity, or multitude. These combine with many prefixes and suffixes to create a number of words. By understanding and learning these prefixes and suffixes, one can understand several unfamiliar numerical words.

LESSON 1.1: NUMBERS

We recognize a *number* as a digit, unit, quantity, or multitude. *Numer* also serves as a root meaning number.

Beginning	Root Word	Ending	New Word	Definition
	number	less	numberless	too many to be counted
re	**number**		renumber	to count again
un	**number**	ed	unnumbered	without count; not counted
	numer	able	numerable	capable of being numbered or counted
	numer	ate	numerate	to count (verb)
	numer	ology	numerology	study of hidden significance in numbers
in	**numer**	able	innumerable	unable to be counted
super	**numer**	ary	supernumerary	what is beyond the number or excessive in number

WEB QUIZ

Instructions: Try your hand at creating words! Connect the correct root word listed in the inner circle to the word parts listed in the outer circles. You may have to use a root word more than once!

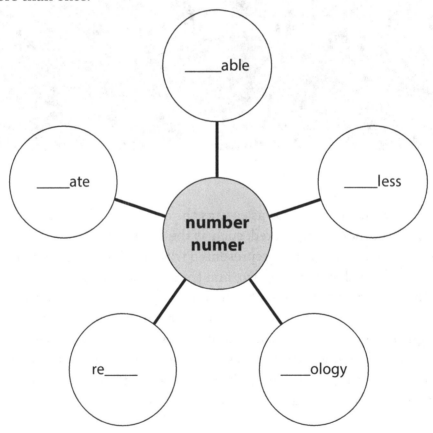

PICK THE WORD

Instructions: Choose the best word or phrase that completes each sentence.

1. Because some of the kids in my class were goofing off, the P.E. teacher lost her place and had to *(numerable, renumber, innumerable)* us for the volleyball teams.

2. The vast sky was filled with *(numerable, renumber, innumerable)* stars, so many that we lost track of them all.

3. My favorite detective often uses *(numerology, numberless, supernumerary)* to help her crack the codes in clues and solve crimes.

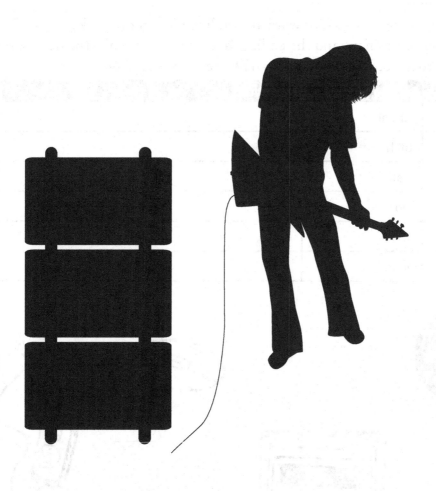

LESSON 1.2: ONE HALF

The Greek root for one half is *hemi*, and the Latin prefixes are *semi* and *demi*. These prefixes tell you when something is incomplete or halved.

Beginning	Root Word	Ending	New Word	Definition
	hemi	plegia	hemiplegia	paralysis in half of the body
	hemi	stitch	hemistitch	half line of verse or poetry
	semi	lunar	semilunar	shaped like a half moon
	semi	annual	semiannual	twice a year
	semi	final	semifinal	next to the last
	semi	detached	semidetached	describing two residences with one wall in common, as in a duplex dwelling
	demi	god	demigod	half-god, half-human, or someone who has attained a god-like fame or status
	demi	john	demijohn	glass or stoneware containers with wicker work
	demi	lune	demilune	half moon, crescent

MAKE A WORD

Instructions: Match the correct root word and ending together to make six words. For example, the root word "non" and the ending "agon" together make the new word "nonagon." The root words and endings can be used more than once.

Root Word	Ending	New Word
hemi	annual	
semi	stitch	
demi	final	
	god	
	plegia	
	lunar	

THINKING ABOUT VOCABULARY

Some ancient Greeks believed that originally humans were in the form of a sphere or circle-shaped with one half male and the other half female. The gods were so angry that the humans lived in such romantic harmony that they split the spheres in half. The "hemispheres" spent their lives searching for their other half, and this was the Greek explanation for the impulse to find a marriage partner.

Instructions: Use the vocabulary in this lesson to answer the following questions.

1. The Earth is also divided into hemispheres. From the Equator, the Earth is divided into Northern and Southern hemispheres. From the Prime Meridian, the Earth is divided into Eastern and Western hemispheres. Using an atlas or globe, figure out which hemispheres you're in right now.

   _____

2. When an event is said to be biennial, it occurs every two years. What would you call an event that happened twice a year?

   _____

3. In the book, *The Lightning Thief*, Perseus Jackson learns that he is a demigod: his mother is mortal and his father is the immortal god, Poseidon. On another piece of paper, write a short story pretending you just found out you were a demigod. How would you react? What would you do first? Would you have any special powers?

LESSON 1.3: ONE

The prefixes *uni* (Latin), *mono* (Greek), and *sol* help determine when a word refers to only one of something, when parts are brought together, and when something applies to all parties.

Beginning	Root Word	Ending	New Word	Definition
	uni	t	unit	single number, or single object
	uni	que	unique	one-of-a-kind
	un(i)	animous	unanimous	total agreement of those involved
	uni	tard	unitard	a single tight garment that covers the torso and sometimes the arms and legs
	mono	logue	monologue	speech or talk by one speaker only
	mono	gram	monogram	several letters combined in one design
	mono	cle	monocle	a corrective lens for one eye only
	mono	tonous	monotonous	describing the same action done repeatedly
	sol	itary	solitary	alone, lone
	sol	itude	solitude	state of being alone
de	**sol**	ate	desolate	left alone; lonely, deserted

WEB QUIZ

Instructions: Try your hand at creating words! Connect the correct root word listed in the inner circle to the word parts listed in the outer circles. You may have to use a root word more than once!

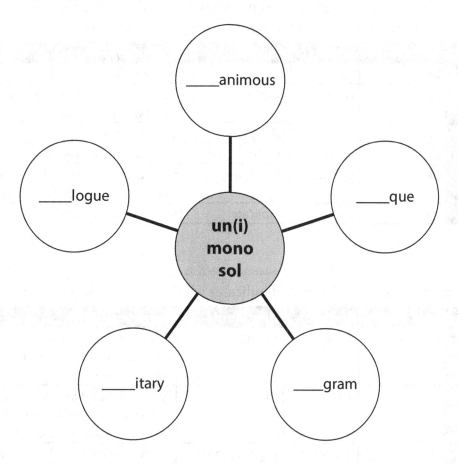

FILL IN THE BLANK

Instructions: Use the words in the tables for Lesson 1.3 to complete the sentences below.

1. Because my brother wouldn't eat his vegetables, he was forced to sit in

   _____ for 5 minutes.

2. Ballerinas and wrestlers often have to wear a _____ as their

   uniform.

3. Her blouse had a pretty _____ on the pocket, displaying her

   initials in pink thread.

4. The election for president of our riding club was _____;

   everyone wanted Sarah to serve in the role.

LESSON 1.4: TWO AND THREE

TWO

The prefixes *bi, di,* and *du* signify two and can help you identify when something is made of or uses two significant parts, happens twice, or has two of something.

Beginning	Root Word	Ending	New Word	Definition
bi	ceps	biceps	muscle with "two heads"
bi	valve	bivalve	having two valves in the heart; a mollusk with two shell halves
bi	lingual	bilingual	speaking two languages
di	oxide	dioxide	compound with two molecules of oxygen
di	phthong	diphthong	two vowels that sound together to make one "hybrid" vowel (e.g., *eu* as in man*eu*ver)
du	plicate	duplicate	to make two or more copies

THREE

The prefix *tri-* comes from Latin and indicates when there is three of something.

Beginning	Root Word	Ending	New Word	Definition
tri	dent	trident	three-pronged spear used by Roman gladiators or wielded by the Greek god of the sea, Poseidon
tri	age	triage	system devised in World War II to sort out wounded soldiers into three groups according to severity of injury
tri	gonometry	trigonometry	mathematical branch based on calculations of kinds of triangles
tri	nity	trinity	a group of three; in Christianity, the three persons of God: Father, Son, and Holy Spirit
tri	bune	tribune	magistrate or head of one of three tribes in ancient Rome; a common newspaper name
tri	be	tribe	first or chief builder or designer
tri	logy	trilogy	group of three stories, novels, films, or dramas

WEB QUIZ

Instructions: Try your hand at creating words! Connect the correct root word listed in the inner circle to the word parts listed in the outer circles. You may have to use a root word more than once!

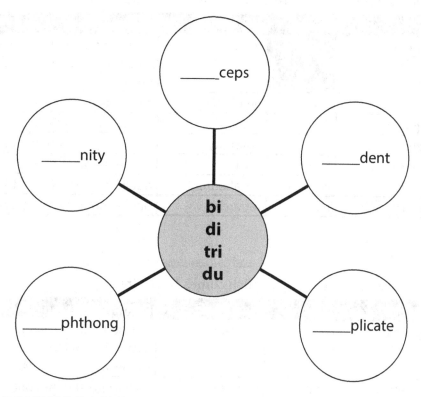

THINKING ABOUT VOCABULARY

In old stories from England to Turkey, we hear of heroes having to complete three tasks. We give three cheers. We get three wishes. Is it mere coincidence?
Instructions: Use the vocabulary in this lesson to answer the following questions.

1. Name a fairy tale, nursery rhyme, or another fictional story that includes three of something.

   _____

2. Triangles form the basis of calculations in what branch of mathematics?

   _____

3. If you could have three wishes, what would they be? (You cannot wish for more wishes!)

   _____

   _____

   _____

LESSON 1.5: FOUR AND FIVE

FOUR

The roots for the number four are *quad*, *quadr*, *quart*, and *tetra*.

Beginning	Root Word	Ending	New Word	Definition
	quad		quad	short for quadrangle or quadruplets; also an area at a college surrounded by buildings on all sides
	quadr	iplegic	quadriplegic	a person whose four limbs are paralyzed
	quadr	ant	quadrant	one fourth of a circle or square
	quart	erly	quarterly	occurring at 3-month intervals
	quat	rain	quatrain	group or stanza of four lines of poetry
	tetra	hedron	tetrahedron	a solid figure with four triangular faces
	tetra	rch	tetrarch	one of four rulers; rule by four

FIVE

The prefix for five is *pent* or *penta*, which comes from Greek.

Beginning	Root Word	Ending	New Word	Definition
	penta	gon	pentagon	a closed shape having five sides and angles; a large U.S. military complex of the same shape in Arlington, VA
	pent	athlon	pentathlon	an ancient athletic contest consisting of five events: jumping, sprinting, discus-throwing, spear-throwing, and wrestling
	pent	ecost	Pentecost	Jewish festival of Shavuot 50 days after Pentecostal Passover, or the Christian celebration anticipating the Holy Spirit

MATCHING

Instructions: Match the root words to their definitions. Definitions can be used more than once.

Root Words
1. Quadr
2. Penta
3. Tetra
4. Quart

Definitions
a. four
b. five

SCRAMBLER

Instructions: Unscramble each word listed below. Use the clues to help you decipher the words.

leatophntn
(contest with five events)

udrntqaa
(one fourth)

carertth
(four rulers)

tiqranua
(four lines of poetry)

earlyqurt
(occurs every three months)

tongpane
(shape with five sides)

Name:_____ Date:_____

LESSON 1.6: SIX, SEVEN, AND EIGHT

SIX

Hexa comes from Greek and Latin words for six; *sex* comes from Latin.

Beginning	Root Word	Ending	New Word	Definition
	hexa	gonal	hexagonal	having the shape of a hexagon
	hexa	chord	hexachord	six-stringed instrument
	sex	tant	sextant	a device with a graduated arc that is equal to one sixth of a circle
	sex	tet	sextet	a musical composition of six parts

SEVEN

The roots for seven are *sept*, which comes from Latin, and *hept*, which means seven in Greek.

Beginning	Root Word	Ending	New Word	Definition
	sept	umvirate	septumvirate	ruling body of seven leaders
	sept	ennial	septennial	occurring every seven years
	hept	ad	heptad	a group of seven
	hept	ahedron	heptahedron	a geometrical solid with seven sides

EIGHT

Oct comes from the Greek for eight.

Beginning	Root Word	Ending	New Word	Definition
	oct	agonal	octagonal	having eight sides and angles
	oct	ane	octane	eight carbon atoms in a hydrocarbon (used in fuels)
	oct	et	octet	a group of eight musicians or the music written for them
	oct	opus	octopus	eight-legged sea animal

Rockin' Root Words Book 2 © Taylor & Francis Group • Permission is granted to photocopy or reproduce this page for single classroom use only.

MORE OR LESS?

Instructions: Look at the sets of words below and choose whether the first word in each set has more or less than the other.

1. **octagonal** (more than, less than) **hexagonal**

2. **sextet** (more than, less than) **octet**

3. **heptad** (more than, less than) **octane**

WEB QUIZ

Instructions: Try your hand at creating words! Connect the correct root word listed in the inner circle to the word parts listed in the outer circles. You may have to use a root word more than once!

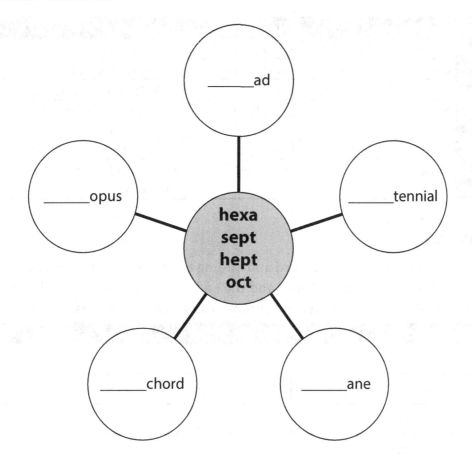

LESSON 1.7: NINE AND TEN

NINE

Non comes from the Latin meaning nine and is used to mean the end of something.

Beginning	Root Word	Ending	New Word	Definition
	non	et	nonet	a musical composition of nine voices or instruments
	non	illion	nonillion	the number one followed by 30 zeroes
	non	es	nones	ninth hour after sunrise, or midday

TEN

Roots for the number ten are *dec* for one tenth and *deca* for ten times from Latin. These roots can be found in the metric system and take many forms in English mathematical vocabulary.

Beginning	Root Word	Ending	New Word	Definition
	dec	ennial	decennial	every 10 years
	dec	imeter	decimeter	one tenth of a meter
	dec	imate	decimate	to destroy; to execute every 10th person
	dec	athlete	decathlete	one participating in a decathlon (10 sporting events)
	deca	gon	decagon	a shape made of 10 angles
	deca	pod	decapod	a 10-legged creature, such as crabs, shrimp, and lobsters

MAKE A WORD

Instructions: Match the correct root word and ending together to make six new words. For example, the root word "non" and the ending "agon" together make the new word "nonagon." The root words and endings can be used more than once.

Root Word	Ending	New Word
non	imeter	
dec	illion	
deca	agenarian	
	imate	
	gon	
	et	

FILL IN THE BLANK

Instructions: Use the words in the tables for Lesson 1.7 to complete the sentences below.

1. The mysterious kid told me to meet him around _____ or

    midday.

2. The defending army was able to _____ the other with its far

    greater firepower and number of troops.

3. I went out for track hoping to become a _____—I was intrigued

    by the idea of competing in 10 events.

LESSON 1.8: ONE HUNDRED AND ONE THOUSAND

ONE HUNDRED

Cent comes from Latin (through French) to mean one hundred of something, as in century.

Beginning	Root Word	Ending	New Word	Definition
	cent	enarian	centenarian	a person at least 100 years old
	cent	urion	centurion	a Roman commander in charge of 100 men
	cent	ennial	centennial	a happening every 100 years
	cent	igrade	centigrade	a scale for measuring temperature in which the freezing and boiling points of water are 100 degrees apart

ONE THOUSAND

Milli, from Latin by way of French, often is used in science, medicine, and industry to show one thousand of something or to indicate a part that is one thousandth of something. Similarly, *kilo* is used to indicate one thousand and derives from Greek via French.

Beginning	Root Word	Ending	New Word	Definition
	milli	on	million	one thousand thousands
	milli	liter	milliliter	1/1,000 of a liter (liquid volume)
	milli	gram	milligram	1/1,000 of a gram (solid volume)
	milli	onaire	millionaire	someone in possession of a million dollars or more
	kilo	byte	kilobyte	one thousand units of computer storage capacity
	kilo	calorie	kilocalorie	one thousand calories
	kilo	hertz	kilohertz	wave frequency of 1,000 cycles per second
	kilo	volt	kilovolt	electrical unit of 1,000 volts

MATCHING

Instructions: Match the root words to their definitions. Definitions can be used more than once.

Root Words

1. kilo
2. milli
3. cent

Definitions

a. one hundred
b. one thousand

ALL MIXED UP

Instructions: Help! The following word parts were all mixed up in the dictionary. Connect the word parts by drawing lines between the boxes. Then, write the correct words in the lines next to their definitions. Be careful! Some of the connections can be tricky: You only want to find words that match the definitions below.

1. _____: wave frequency of 1,000 cycles per second

2. _____: someone who is at least 100 years old

3. _____: one thousand units of computer storage

4. _____: $\frac{1}{1000}$ of a liter

5. _____: Roman commander in charge of 100 men

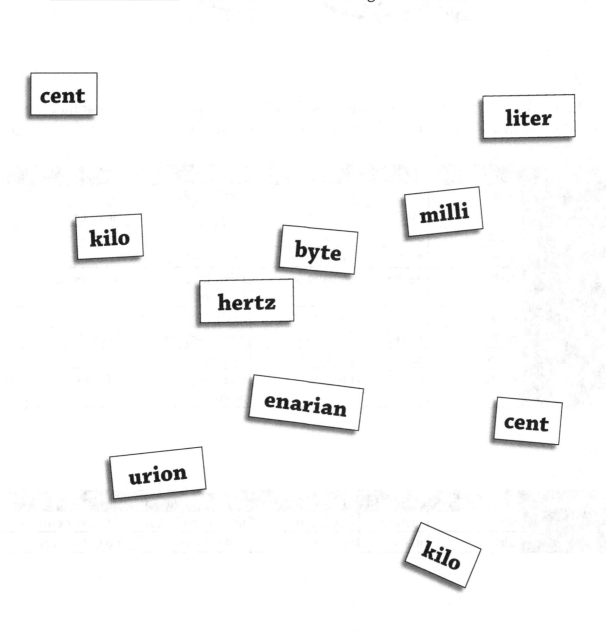

cent

liter

milli

kilo

byte

hertz

enarian

cent

urion

kilo

LESSON 1.9: FIRST AND LAST

WELL, WELL, WELL... IF IT ISN'T MY OLD ARCH-ENEMY!

FIRST

Prim (Latin), *arch* (French, Latin, and Greek), and *proto* (Greek) are roots that indicate something as first in a sequence, the main focus, or the leader or chief of a project or group of people.

Beginning	Root Word	Ending	New Word	Definition
	prim	e	prime	first in rank, chief, main
	prim	itive	primitive	from early times; simple or crude
	prim	adonna	primadonna	first lady or a temperamental person
	prim	eval	primeval	of ancient ages
	arch	aeology	archaeology	scientific study of ancient people and customs
	arch	aic	archaic	ancient or old-fashioned
	arch	etype	archetype	first mold, pattern, or model
	proto	zoa	protozoa	first animals; microscopic creatures
	proto	n	proton	first ion; positive part of the nucleus of an atom

LAST

Ulti comes from Latin.

Beginning	Root Word	Ending	New Word	Definition
	ulti	matum	ultimatum	final condition, stipulation, or demand
	ulti	macy	ultimacy	state or quality of being last to finish

WORD SPLITS

Instructions: The makers of a new dictionary want to break up some words into their word parts for their new edition, but need your help! Can you divide the following words into their word parts? Think carefully—a few words may be new to you!

1. primadonna: _____ + _____

2. proton: _____ + _____

3. penultimate: _____ + _____ + _____

4. archaic: _____ + _____

5. archaeologist: _____ + _____

WHAT DOESN'T BELONG?

Instructions: Choose the word in each line that *does not* mean the same as the first word.

1. **ultimacy**   last   final   first

2. **prime**   first   secondary   chief

3. **primitive**   simple   crude   modern

4. **archetype**   first impression   finished product   model

5. **ultimatum**   final demand   final draft   final condition

CHAPTER I REVIEW

NUMBER SENSE

Instructions: You've been assigned to create two bulletin boards of vocabulary words related to numbers for an extra credit project when a strong gust of wind blows through the windows, scattering your words everywhere! From the word bank, select the words that correspond to each number on the bulletin boards and write them in the blanks for each number.

Word Bank: duplicate, kilovolt, septumvirate, trinity, decapod, sextant, quadriplegic, monocle, heptad, nonet, tetrahedron, bivalve, trident, pentagon, decennial, octane, milligram, hexachord, unit, centigrade

CHAPTER 2

Quantifiers and Size

Aside from our sense of good, bad, and neutral, nothing shapes the way we look at the world around us more than our sense of quantity. From the time we are babies, quantity words fall into three general categories: none, one, and some. Many quantity words will be familiar to you as a result.

We also cover words dealing with size in this chapter. As we know, people tend to exaggerate, so naturally our language has a great number of words to describe the relative largeness or smallness of objects. Many of these words have been pulled from Latin and Greek.

LESSON 2.1: EQUAL

The prefixes for equality are *iso* (Greek) and *equ/equi* (Latin). They have many uses in mathematical language and can pinpoint equality or sameness.

Beginning	Root Word	Ending	New Word	Definition
	iso	tope	isotope	having equal place on the periodic table of chemical elements
	iso	sceles	isosceles	equal legs of a triangle
	iso	metry	isometry	equality of measure
	equ	ality	equality	the condition of being equal
	equ	ate	equate	to make equal
	equ	ation	equation	a statement of equality between two quantities
	equi	librium	equilibrium	state of balance between two opposite forces
	equi	valent	equivalent	equal in quantity, force, value, or meaning

WEB QUIZ

Instructions: Try your hand at creating words! Connect the correct root word listed in the inner circle to the word parts listed in the outer circles. You may have to use a root word more than once!

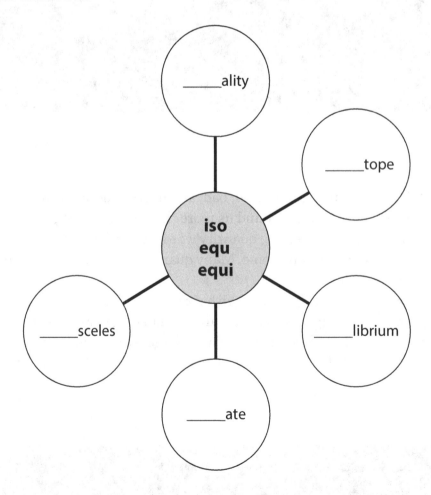

FILL IN THE BLANK

Instructions: Use the words for Lesson 2.1 to complete the sentences below.

1. By making each team member responsible for one of the trivia questions, our coach developed a sense of _____ among us regarding the game's outcome.

2. With the loss of one key player, the two basketball teams were unable to reach a state of _____; one team dominated the second half.

3. "Today we will be working with two chemicals that are _____ or equals on the periodic table," my chemistry teacher announced.

4. She ensured that the two lanes on the track showed _____; they were both measured to be equal distances.

5. My math homework included a particularly difficult _____ that I struggled to solve.

LESSON 2.2: BOTH AND NONE

BOTH

Knowing the prefixes *ambi*, *amph*, and *amphi* can help you understand words referring to both, both sides, or surrounding (on both sides).

Beginning	Root Word	Ending	New Word	Definition
	ambi	guous	ambiguous	having two meanings, confusing, doubtful
	ambi	dextrous	ambidextrous	describing one who can use both hands equally efficiently
	ambi	valence	ambivalence	state of being uncommitted to either side
	amphi	theater	amphitheater	a theater in which the seats surround the stage
	amph	ora	amphora	a jar with two handles, one on each side

NONE

Neg comes from Latin, meaning no or none.

Beginning	Root Word	Ending	New Word	Definition
	neg	ate	negate	to deny the existence or truth of something
	neg	ative	negative	no; in numbers, less than zero
	neg	lect	neglect	to ignore or disregard
	neg	ligible	negligible	small or unimportant, easily neglected
re	neg	ade	renegade	an outlaw or rebel

MATCHING

Instructions: Match the root words to their definitions. Definitions can be used more than once.

Root Words
1. ambi
2. neg
3. amph

Definitions
a. none
b. both

SYNONYM SEARCH

Instructions: Sort through the words in the word bank to find synonyms for the vocabulary words listed below. Write the synonyms on the lines next to the words they correspond with. Be careful—some of the words in the word bank will not be used!

Word Bank: ignore, certain, uncommitted, use both hands, confusing, unimportant, outlaw, outdoor theater, deny

1. ambidextrous _____

2. renegade _____

3. negate _____

4. neglect _____

5. ambivalence _____

LESSON 2.3: MANY

The prefixes for many are *plu and plur* (Latin through French), *multi* (Latin), and *poly* (Greek).

Beginning	Root Word	Ending	New Word	Definition
	plu	s	plus	add, gain
	plur	ilingual	plurilingual	to speak more than one language
	multi	cellular	multicellular	animals with many cells
	multi	form	multiform	having many shapes
	multi	national	multinational	of or involving many nations
	poly	gon	polygon	a shape with many angles
	poly	graph	polygraph	a machine used in crime detection that records many things at one time
	poly	mer	polymer	synthetic substance made of giant molecules joined together

MAKE A WORD

Instructions: Match the correct root word and ending together to make five words. For example, the root word "non" and the ending "agon" together make the word "nonagon." The root words and endings can be used more than once.

Root Word	Ending	New Word
plu	mer	
plur	s	
multi	gon	
poly	national	
	ilingual	

CHANGE IT UP

Instructions: Replace the underlined word or words in each sentence with one of the vocabulary words in the word bank.

Word Bank: polygraph, multiform, plurilingual, polygon

1. In art class, we created a <u>many shaped</u> sculpture to show our geometrical knowledge.
2. I want to learn French to be <u>able to speak more than one language</u>.
3. A pentagon is an example of a <u>shape with many angles</u>.
4. To determine the perpetrator, a <u>machine that measures many things at once</u> was administered, revealing who was lying.

LESSON 2.4: ALL/FULL

The prefixes for all and full are *cop* (Latin), *pan* (Greek), and *holo* (Greek, through Latin and French). These prefixes tell you that a word deals with satisfaction, abundance, and wholeness.

Beginning	Root Word	Ending	New Word	Definition
	cop	ious	copious	very plentiful, abundant
cornu	**cop**	ia	cornucopia	horn of plenty, an overflowing fullness
	pan	orama	panorama	complete, all-around view of a scene
	pan	tomime	pantomime	mimic or imitator; a drama or play without words
	pan	demonium	pandemonium	a state of wild uproar
	holo	caust	Holocaust	a whole, burnt offering; the mass destruction of European Jews during World War II
	holo	graph	holograph	a whole document written by hand
cat	**hol**	ic	Catholic	of a church considered "universal"; of wide-ranging tastes

WEB QUIZ

Instructions: Try your hand at creating words! Connect the correct root word listed in the inner circle to the word parts listed in the outer circles. You may have to use a root word more than once!

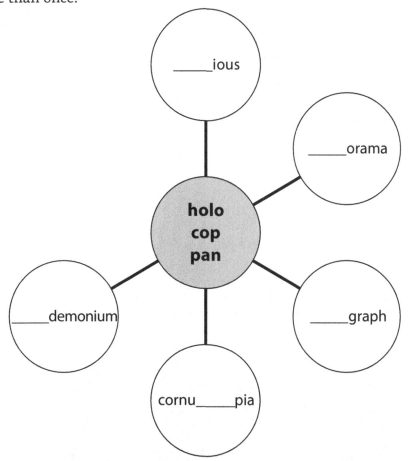

FILL IN THE BLANK

Instructions: Use the words for Lesson 2.4 to complete the sentences below.

1. The classroom looked like a _____ after we filled it with all of the canned goods we had collected.

2. In theater class, we worked in pairs to create a _____ of our favorite fairy tales.

3. Before the printing press was invented, many monks would copy books out by hand, creating valuable and beautiful _____ of popular texts.

4. Anne Frank's diary was found after the end of the _____ and details her experience as a Jewish citizen trying to hide from the Nazi occupiers of Amsterdam.

5. By standing at the top of the mountain, I had a _____, or complete, view of the valley below.

LESSON 2.5: SMALL

Min and *mini* come from the Italian word, *miniatura*. *Micro* comes from Greek and is commonly used in scientific terminology. Both of these root words pertain to small size or to making less.

Beginning	Root Word	Ending	New Word	Definition
	min	ce	mince	to chop something into small pieces
	min	ute	minute	1/60th of an hour; something tiny
	min	utiae	minutiae	finest points of detail
di	**min**	ish	diminish	to make small
	mini	mum	minimum	least quantity possible or permissible
	mini	mize	minimize	to make small in importance or size
	micro	organism	microorganism	a tiny microscopic form of life
	micro	biology	microbiology	study of small life or microorganisms
	micro	nesia	Micronesia	group of small islands in the Pacific Ocean
	micro	chip	microchip	tiny electronic chip used in computers

WEB QUIZ

Instructions: Try your hand at creating words! Connect the correct root word listed in the inner circle to the word parts listed in the outer circles. You may have to use a root word more than once!

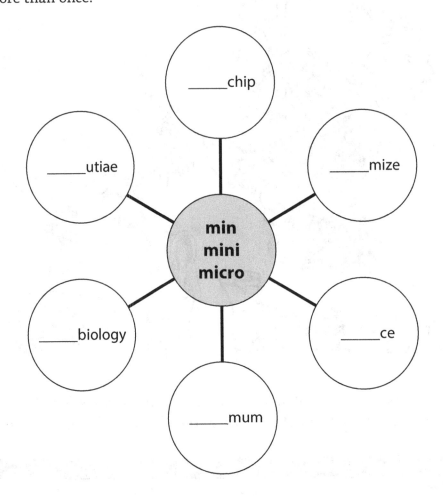

ADDING SUFFIXES AND PREFIXES

Instructions: The suffix "ize" means "to make." Minimize means to make something smaller. Likewise, the prefix "mini" also means something smaller than normal. Using that knowledge, write a possible definition for each of the new words below.

1. legalize _____

2. miniskirt _____

3. authorize _____

4. individualize _____

5. minibus _____

LESSON 2.6: LARGE

The roots *magn* (Latin), *maxi* (Latin), and *macro* (Greek) indicate a word meaning largeness, greatness, length, or of great scope.

Beginning	Root Word	Ending	New Word	Definition
	magn	a Carta	Magna Carta	"great charter" of rights demanded by some English nobles and signed by King John in 1215 C.E.
	magn	ate	magnate	great and powerful person
	magn	um opus	magnum opus	a great work of art, the greatest of one's achievements
	magn	animous	magnanimous	great-hearted, noble in mind, generous
	magn	itude	magnitude	great size, extent, or importance
	maxi	mal	maximal	greatest or highest possible
	maxi	mize	maximize	to make something the biggest or greatest it can be
	macro	cosm	macrocosm	universe as a whole
	macro	nutrient	macronutrient	nutrients needed in large quantities
	macro	scopic	macroscopic	able to be seen by the naked eye

MAKE A WORD
. . . .

Instructions: Match the correct root word and ending together to make five words. For example, the root word "non" and the ending "agon" together make the word "nonagon." The root words and endings can be used more than once.

Root Word	Ending	New Word
magn	scopic	
maxi	ate	
macro	animous	
	mal	
	nutrient	

PICK THE WORD

Instructions: Choose the best word or phrase that completes each sentence.

1. Telescopes bring us closer to the (*macrocosm, macronutrient, microcosm*) that is the Milky Way.

2. I am going to (*maximal, maximize, minimize*) my academic potential by studying for an hour each night.

3. Like Andrew Carnegie and other late 19th-century plutocrats, Donald Trump can be considered a (*magnum opus, magnitude, magnate*) of the business and real estate industries.

4. As I stood at its base looking up, I could not believe the (*magnum opus, magnitude, magnate*) of the Empire State Building.

LESSON 2.7: TALL/LONG AND SHORT/LOW

I PLAY TENOR, HANK PLAYS ALTO, AND THAT'S LEROY ON THE BASS.

TALL/LONG

The roots for tall or long are *long*, *alti* or *alto* (Latin), and *acro* (Greek). These roots make up a number of scientific terms for length or height or for the extremities of the body.

Beginning	Root Word	Ending	New Word	Definition
	long	evity	longevity	a long span of life
e	**long**	ate	elongate	to make longer
ob	**long**		oblong	of elongated shape
	alti	meter	altimeter	instrument for measuring heights above ground or sea level
	acro	phobia	acrophobia	fear of heights
	acro	stic	acrostic	poem in which the first letter of each line spells out a word

SHORT/LOW

Roots for short or low are *brev* (Latin through French) and *bass/bas* (French). Knowing these roots helps you understand when a word pertains to a short duration, the shortening of an item, or a lowness of tone or situation.

Beginning	Root Word	Ending	New Word	Definition
	brev	e	breve	a mark placed over a short or unstressed syllable
ab	**brev**	iate	abbreviate	to make small, summarize
	bass	o	basso	a person who sings very low notes; low in music
	bas	e	base	of low character; undesirable; also that which something else stands upon
de	**bas**	e	debase	to lower the status of or devalue

WORD SPLITS

Instructions: The makers of a new dictionary want to break up some words into their word parts for their new edition, but need your help! Can you divide the following words into their word parts? Think carefully—a few words may be new to you!

1. debase: _____ + _____ + _____

2. acrostic: _____ + _____

3. elongate: _____ + _____ + _____

4. abase: _____ + _____ + _____

5. prolong: _____ + _____

THINKING ABOUT VOCABULARY

In ancient Greek city-states, the Acropolis was the highest point. It was where priests prayed to the gods and sacrifices were made for the good of the city. The wealthiest citizens lived on the hills, while the commoners lived in low-lying areas and on farmland surrounding the city. These areas came to be known as *suburbs* (that is, "below the city") or land below the urban centers.

Instructions: Using the vocabulary from this lesson, answer the questions below.

1. If someone is afraid of spiders, it's called arachnophobia. What is it called when someone is afraid of heights?

    _____

2. Using what you've learned in this lesson and your dictionary, find the definitions of the following words and then write each of them in a new sentence on another piece of paper: basement, bassoon, brevity.

3. The Greek Parthenon rested in the Acropolis of Athens and its ruins continue to be a point of interest for tourists today. With permission from your parents or teacher, find pictures of the Parthenon in Greece. Then, on another piece of paper, create a postcard that shows the Parthenon. Don't forget to caption your postcard with information about this tourist site!

CHAPTER 2 REVIEW

ROOT WORD PYRAMID

Instructions: You've discovered a rare root word pyramid, but it's falling down! Fill in the missing pieces to the pyramid by completing the information in each block using the word bank. Read each block carefully: Some of the blocks require that you fill in the definitions for your vocabulary words and some require that you add the missing vocabulary word.

Word Bank: summarize, isosceles, ambiguous, generous, diminish, multinational, abundant, unimportant, details, maximal

minutiae = finest
_____

abbreviate =
_____

_____
= greatest possible

_____ =
equal legs of a triangle

magnanimous =
_____

negligible =
_____

copious =
_____

_____
= having two meanings

_____
= to make small

_____
= involving many nations

CHAPTER 3

Time

Time is one of the most important factors in our lives. You have to wake up at a certain time to go to school. Recess is for a short time. At the conclusion of the school day, there is a time to go home and finish your homework. There are clocks everywhere. You cannot be late for school, just as your parents cannot be late for their jobs or appointments. Even early humans were aware of time—evidenced by inventions such as the astrolabe and sundial and concepts like day and night or the time from one full moon to the next. The first section of this chapter deals with words associated with periods of time. The second section deals with our measurement of time.

LESSON 3.1: TIME

The roots for time are *temp* and *tempor* (Latin through French) and *chron/cron* (Greek and Latin) and give you a clue about when a word refers to the past, to the impermanence of time, or to the sequence of time.

Beginning	Root Word	Ending	New Word	Definition
	temp	o	tempo	time, rate of movement, or activity in music
	temp	est	tempest	violent storm
con	**tempor**	ary	contemporary	living or happening at the same time
ex	**tempor**	e	extempore	speaking without an outline or a written speech
	chron	ology	chronology	a sequential order of past events
	chron	ic	chronic	lasting a long time or recurring often
syn	**chron**	ized	synchronized	happening at the same time, the state of being set to occur at the same time
	cron	y	crony	an old friend or a dishonest association

WEB QUIZ

Instructions: Try your hand at creating words! Connect the correct root word listed in the inner circle to the word parts listed in the outer circles. You may have to use a root word more than once!

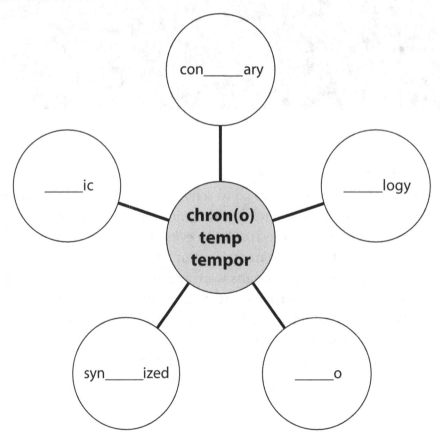

Rockin' Root Words Book 2 © Taylor & Francis Group • Permission is granted to photocopy or reproduce this page for single classroom use only.

THINKING ABOUT VOCABULARY

Kronos was the Greek god of time, and he had a nasty habit of eating his children. His wife had enough of her children being treated like after-dinner mints, and she tricked Kronos by giving him a stone wrapped in a blanket, which he promptly ate. In doing so, she saved her son Zeus, who became the king of the gods and eventually destroyed Kronos.

Instructions: Use the vocabulary in the lesson to answer the following questions.

1. Kronos was the Greek god of time. Name another myth, fable, or fairy tale in which time plays an important role in the story. Explain how time plays a role in this story.

   _____

   _____

   _____

2. What is another term for a dishonest association?

   _____

3. Tempo is often used to determine the *pace* of music. What is another activity that requires you to keep up a tempo, or pace?

   _____

LESSON 3.2: BEFORE

Three prefixes from Latin help you determine when a word's meaning is *before* something else: *fore* for before in time or in front of and *pre* and *ante* for before, in front of, or earlier.

Beginning	Root Word	Ending	New Word	Definition
	fore	warned	forewarned	warned beforehand
	fore	father	forefather	ancestor, literally or metaphorically
	fore	most	foremost	first, most important
	fore	sight	foresight	knowledge of things to come
	fore	boding	foreboding	a sense that horrible events are going to occur
	pre	cede	precede	to come before
	pre	sume	presume	to take for granted
	pre	judice	prejudice	to judge beforehand; hasty opinion based on little knowledge
	pre	monition	premonition	a sense of knowing the future
	ante	bellum	antebellum	before the war

MATCHING

Instructions: Match the words to their definitions.

Words	Definitions
1. forefather	a. before the war
2. antebellum	b. warned beforehand
3. precede	c. ancestor
4. presume	d. sense that horrible things will occur
5. foreboding	e. to come before
6. forewarned	f. take for granted

WHAT DOESN'T BELONG?

Instructions: Choose the word in each line that *does not* mean the same as the first word.

1. **foremost**   most important   final   first

2. **prejudice**   informed decision   judge beforehand   hasty opinion

3. **knowledge of what's to come**   foresight   premonition   foremost

LESSON 3.3: AFTER

The prefixes for afterwards in time are *post* (Latin) and *sec/secut/sequ*.

Beginning	Root Word	Ending	New Word	Definition
	post	bellum	postbellum	after the war
	post	humous	posthumous	after death
	post	secondary	postsecondary	stages of education/life after high school is completed
	post	date	postdate	to assign a date later than the current one
con	**secut**	ive	consecutive	one right after the other
	sequ	el	sequel	that which follows, a successor
	sequ	ential	sequential	following in order
con	**sequ**	ent	consequent	following as a result

WEB QUIZ

Instructions: Try your hand at creating words! Connect the correct root word listed in the inner circle to the word parts listed in the outer circles. You may have to use a root word more than once!

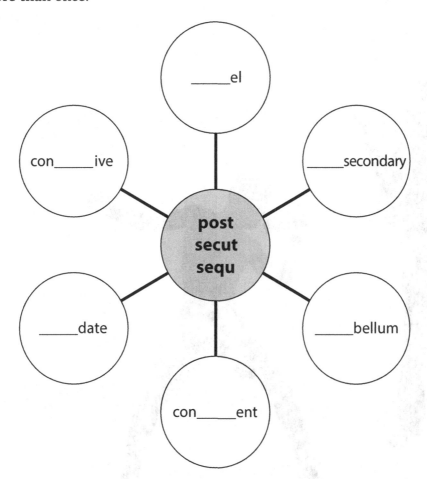

FILL IN THE BLANK

Instructions: Use the words for Lesson 3.3 to complete the sentences below.

1. I had to _____ my essay, as it wasn't due for another week.

2. The _____ for the movie *Iron Man* comes out this summer.

3. Numbers that are _____ are defined as following "one right after another."

4. I made the decision to attend my local state college in order to receive my _____ education.

5. Because she admitted to the vandalism, she had to face the _____ punishment for her actions.

LESSON 3.4: DAY AND NIGHT

DAY

Journ comes from French to mean day, while *dia* comes from Greek to take on the additional meanings of passing through, light, and the passage of the day.

Beginning	Root Word	Ending	New Word	Definition
	dia	ry	diary	daily written record
	dia	l	dial	sundial, face of a clock
meri	**dia**	n	meridian	midday or noontime
	journ	al	journal	a diary with daily entries; a collection of essays written by scholars in a field
	journ	alism	journalism	the practice of writing mostly articles for newspapers or magazines
ad	**journ**		adjourn	to end a meeting; to put off or suspend
so	**journ**		sojourn	a journey

NIGHT

Noct comes from Latin through French and *nox* comes from Latin to mean night. *Nox* carries the additional meanings of harm, injury, or offense (like obnoxious).

Beginning	Root Word	Ending	New Word	Definition
	noct	urnal	nocturnal	pertaining to nighttime
	noct	urne	nocturne	musical night piece or a painting showing a night scene
equi	**nox**		equinox	two days each year when the days and nights are equal

WORD SPLITS

Instructions: The makers of a new dictionary want to break up some words into their word parts for their new edition, but need your help! Can you divide the following words into their word parts? Think carefully—a few words may be new to you!

1. equinox: _____ + _____

2. journey: _____ + _____

3. meridian: _____ + _____ + _____

4. journalist: _____ + _____

5. nocturne: _____ + _____

ALL MIXED UP

Instructions: Help! The following word parts were all mixed up in the dictionary. Connect the word parts by drawing lines between the boxes. Then, write the correct words in the lines next to their definitions. Be careful! Some of the connections can be tricky: You only want to find words that match the definitions below.

1. _____: daily written record

2. _____: collection of essays

3. _____: pertaining to nighttime

4. _____: to put off

5. _____: face of a clock

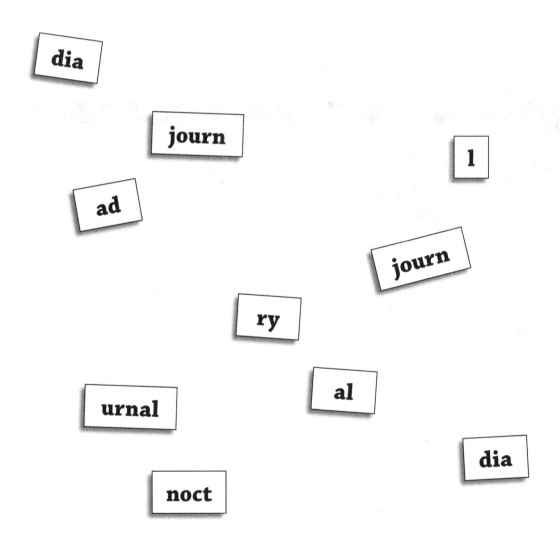

LESSON 3.5: MONTH

LUNA-TICK

Mon is a root for month or the time it takes for the moon to change from one full moon to the next. *Luna* comes from Latin through French and carries an additional meaning of insanity. *Mest* also can stand for month.

Beginning	Root Word	Ending	New Word	Definition
	mon	day	Monday	day of the moon, from Old English
	mon	thly	monthly	occurring once a month
	mon	th	month	period of time between two full moons
	luna	r	lunar	of or belonging to the moon
	luna	te	lunate	crescent-shaped or moon-shaped
	luna	cy	lunacy	moon-struck condition, a state of madness
	luna	tic	lunatic	one who suffers from madness; in earlier times, it was thought people lost their minds due to a full moon
se	**mest**	er	semester	pertaining to half an academic year or to a period of 6 months

MAKE A WORD

Instructions: Match the correct root word and ending together to make five words. For example, the root word "non" and the ending "agon" together make the word "nonagon." The root words and endings can be used more than once.

Root Word	Ending	New Word
mon	thly	
luna	te	
	tic	
	th	
	r	

FILL IN THE BLANK

Instructions: Use the words for Lesson 3.5 to complete the sentences below.

1. I always get the blues on _____ when I have to go back to school after the weekend.

2. The attorney tried to plead the defendant's fits of _____ as an explanation for his crimes.

3. Many colleges are on the _____ system, with the majority of classes being taken in the spring and fall.

4. The small, _____ scar looked just like a bite mark with its crescent shape and raised edges.

5. I had to visit the doctor _____; he had to check the progress of my treatment every 4 weeks.

LESSON 3.6: YEAR

The roots *ann* and *enn* come from Latin and indicate something that marks the year or years.

Beginning	Root Word	Ending	New Word	Definition
	ann	ual	annual	yearly
	ann	uity	annuity	fixed yearly payment or pension
	ann	als	annals	annual books or records
per	**enn**	ial	perennial	yearly
bicent	**enn**	ial	bicentennial	every 200 years
bi	**enn**	ial	biennial	every 2 years
cent	**enn**	ial	centennial	every 100 years
mill	**enn**	ial	millennial	every 1,000 years

MORE OFTEN OR LESS OFTEN?

Instructions: Look at the sets of words below and choose whether the first word in each set occurs more often or less often than the other.

1. **millennial** (more often than, less often than) **centennial**

2. **perennial** (more often than, less often than) **biennial**

3. **centennial** (more often than, less often than) **bicentennial**

WEB QUIZ

Instructions: Try your hand at creating words! Connect the correct root word listed in the inner circle to the word parts listed in the outer circles. You may have to use a root word more than once!

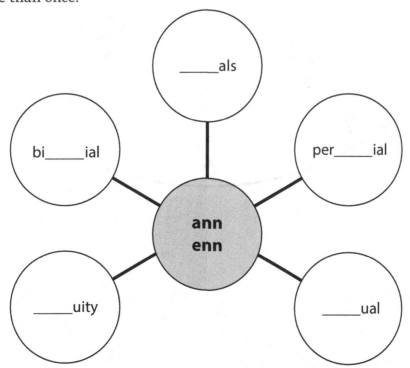

CHAPTER 3 REVIEW

THE WORD CLOCK

Instructions: Use the definitions on each section of the clock to help you fill in the missing words.

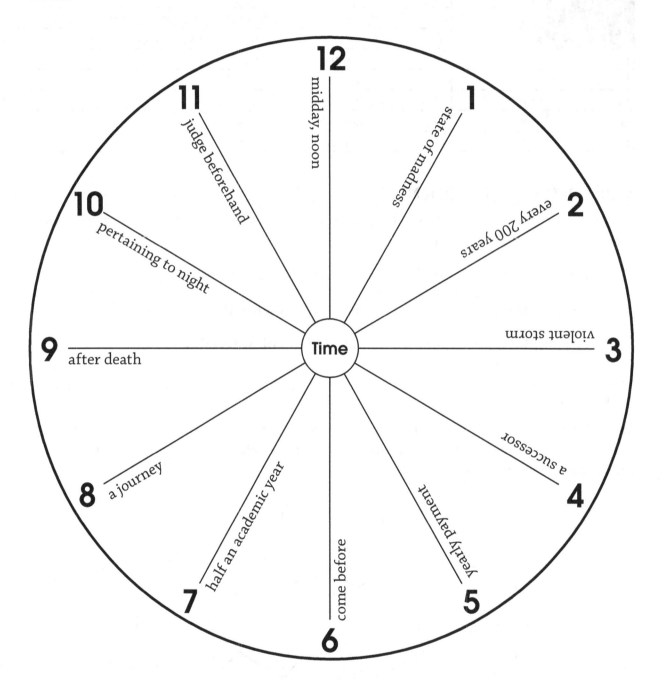

CHAPTER 4

Location, Directions, and Relationships

Good directions are helpful in finding a location, but what is a location? A location is where an object or person can be found and it is described with words such as up, ahead of, next to, or below. When you recognize and understand these words, you can find anything! Direction is simply the location of two objects, places, or people in relationship to each other. Directions guide us from one location to another.

LESSON 4.1: ABOVE

The roots that mean above are *epi* (Greek), *super* (Latin), *over* and *out* (Middle English), and *hyper*. These roots note when a word refers to being on something, completeness, excessiveness, or being beyond or more than what is normal.

Beginning	Root Word	Ending	New Word	Definition
	epi	dermis	epidermis	outer layer of skin
	epi	demic	epidemic	widespread disease affecting many people; uncontrollable spread of illness
	super	stition	superstition	belief in supernatural occurrences
	super	b	superb	of highest quality
	over	board	overboard	excessive
	over	throw	overthrow	to take over, usually with violence
	out	rage	outrage	great anger
	out	ward	outward	on the outside
	hyper	active	hyperactive	overactive
	hyper	bole	hyperbole	an extravagant exaggeration

WEB QUIZ

Instructions: Try your hand at creating words! Connect the correct root word listed in the inner circle to the word parts listed in the outer circles. You may have to use a root word more than once!

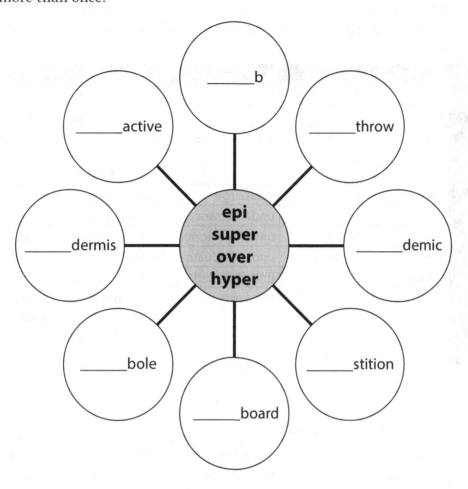

FILL IN THE BLANK

Instructions: Use the words for Lesson 4.1 to complete the sentences below.

1. I believe in the _____ that if you break a mirror you have bad luck for 7 years.

2. My brother and his friends were so _____ that my mom finally had to separate them to keep them from bouncing all over the house.

3. I heard on the news that a tribe in Africa attempted to _____ another tribe's leader in order to gain its resources.

4. We had to get the H1N1 shots at school to help control the spread of a flu _____.

LESSON 4.2: BELOW

Sub comes from Latin and gives meaning to words like submerge and subdivision. *Under* comes from Old English and defines something that does not meet expectations or is below the standard in some way. *Hyp* and *hypo* come from Greek and are typically used with medical words.

Beginning	Root Word	Ending	New Word	Definition
	sub	terranean	subterranean	underground
	sub	standard	substandard	below standard or of inferior quality
	sub	conscious	subconscious	in psychology, the consciousness that our minds have no access to, but that governs many of our drives or desires
	sub	merge	submerge	to dip or immerse in water
	under	current	undercurrent	an underlying force
	under	developed	underdeveloped	not sufficiently developed
	under	graduate	undergraduate	college student who has not yet graduated
	under	handed	underhanded	secret, sly, deceitful
	hypo	crisy	hypocrisy	act of pretending to be what one is not or of recommending something to others and doing the opposite
	hypo	thermia	hypothermia	condition of lowered body temperature

THINKING ABOUT VOCABULARY

Looking at the root words for below, is it any surprise that the train system that takes passengers *under* a city like New York City or London is called the *sub*way? *Sub* and *under* are two root words used in much of our culture and everyday language. Fill in the boxes below to suggest additional common words that use *sub* or *under* as their roots.

sub
_____
_____
_____

under
_____
_____
_____

WEB QUIZ

Instructions: Try your hand at creating words! Connect the correct root word listed in the inner circle to the word parts listed in the outer circles. You may have to use a root word more than once!

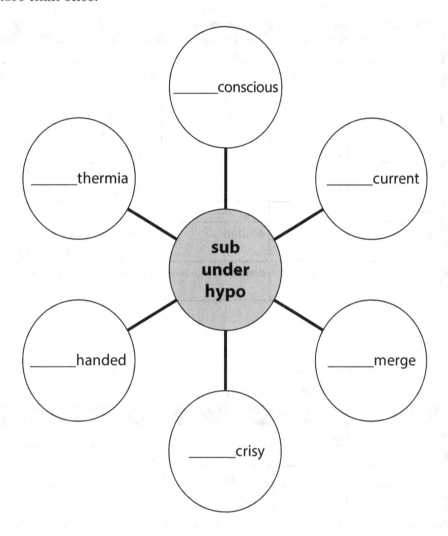

Name:_____ Date:_____

LESSON 4.3: INSIDE AND OUTSIDE

The prefixes for inside are *in*, *intra* (Latin), *intro*, and *en/em* (Greek). These roots signify a meaning that is interior, turning inward, detailing, or summoning from within.

Beginning	Root Word	Ending	New Word	Definition
	in	spect	inspect	look into carefully
	in	scription	inscription	a mark or engraving; a dedication written in a book
	intra	mural	intramural	conducted or situated inside the walls of a building or institution
	intro	spect	introspect	to look inward
	intro	vert	introvert	in psychology, one with inward thoughts; someone with a shy, contemplative nature
	en	grave	engrave	to carve in or on
	em	bark	embark	to take goods or passengers aboard a ship; to begin a journey or task
	em	pathy	empathy	identification with the feelings of another person

OUTSIDE

The roots for outside are *e*, *ex*, *exo*, *ec*, and *ecto*. They are from Greek and Latin and refer to something going out, obliterated, removed, or outside of what is considered normal.

Beginning	Root Word	Ending	New Word	Definition
	e	radicate	eradicate	erase; obliterate
	e	gress	egress	to go out or exit
	ex	tinguish	extinguish	wipe out; obliterate
	ex	cavate	excavate	to make hollow; to dig out an archaeological site
	ec	lipse	eclipse	an overshadowing, as during a solar or lunar eclipse
append	ec	tomy	appendectomy	surgical removal of the appendix
	ecto	derm	ectoderm	outside layers of skin

MATCHING

Instructions: Match the root words to their definitions. Definitions can be used more than once.

Root Words

1. in
2. em
3. ecto
4. intro
5. ex
6. e

Definitions

a. inside
b. outside

OUTSIDE OR INSIDE?

Instructions: Using the words in this lesson and your dictionary, decide which words in the word bank go with each definition. Then, write the words referring to "inside" in the center of the circle. Place the words referring to "outside" on the outside of the circle. Use this graphic organizer to help you the next time you need to remember the difference between "inside" and "outside" words. Be careful! Some of the words may be new to you!

Word Bank: index, engrave, introspect, eradicate, eject, exhale, embassy, excavate

1. to look inwards
2. safe house for citizens of one country located inside another country
3. to obliterate
4. to carve in or on
5. to breathe out
6. to throw or force out
7. a listing of the topics contained within a book
8. to make hollow

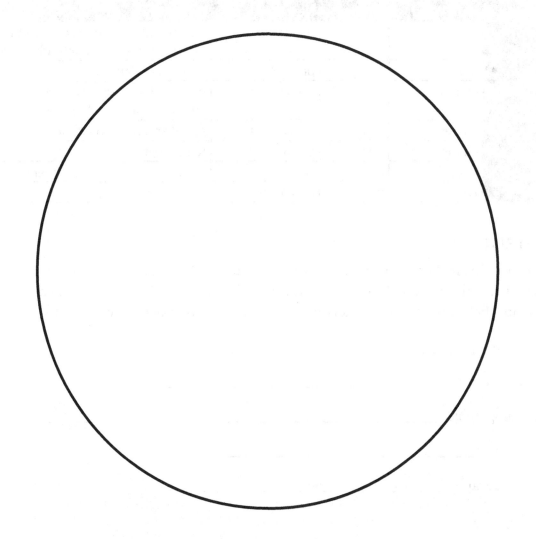

LESSON 4.4: BESIDE/ALONGSIDE AND AROUND

BESIDE/ALONGSIDE

Para comes from Greek and can help determine when a word's meaning is beside or alongside something else or something that is distinct.

Beginning	Root Word	Ending	New Word	Definition
para	llelogram	parallelogram	a shape with at least two parallel sides
para	meter	parameter	a variable mathematical constant used to determine other variables
para	ble	parable	a story meant to illustrate a moral or religious principle
para	dox	paradox	statement that seems contrary to logic, but may in fact be true
para	digm	paradigm	a pattern, example, or model

AROUND

The prefix forms for round are *peri* (Greek) and *circu/circum* (Latin).

Beginning	Root Word	Ending	New Word	Definition
peri	scope	periscope	instrument used to look above the surface of water while remaining submerged
peri	phery	periphery	outer boundary, perimeter
circum	stance	circumstance	the position in which one finds oneself; a fact or event related to another
circum	vent	circumvent	to get around an obstacle
circum	scribe	circumscribe	to set limits
circu	it	circuit	a complete electrical or other loop
circu	itous	circuitous	roundabout, indirect

WORD SPLITS

Instructions: The makers of a new dictionary want to break up some words into their word parts for their new edition, but need your help! Can you divide the following words into their word parts? Think carefully—a few words may be new to you!

1. periscope: _____ + _____

2. circumscribe: _____ + _____

3. comparable: _____ + _____ + _____

4. circuit: _____ + _____

5. paragraph: _____ + _____

PICK THE WORD

Instructions: Choose the best word or phrase that completes each sentence.

1. A story that illustrates a *(scene, moral, landscape)*, like those in the Bible or *Aesop's Fables*, is called a parable.

2. My teacher suggested that when we paint, we stay inside the *(periscope, parameter, periphery)* of the canvas.

3. The beltway surrounding Atlanta, I-285, is circuitous; therefore it is a(n) *(direct, indirect, straightforward)* way to get from one side of the city to another.

4. My grandmother instilled in me that I can *(circumvent, circumscribe, circumstance)* any obstacles in life.

LESSON 4.5: TOWARD/TO AND AWAY

TOWARD/TO

Ad acts as a prefix when it is attached to a verb. It means direction toward, but it combines in different ways to produce different meanings with different consonants. Other prefixes meaning toward/to include *af, ag, al,* and *an.*

Beginning	Root Word	Ending	New Word	Definition
ad	apt		adapt	to change habits to fit a given situation
ad	vance		advance	to move forward
af	fluent		affluent	wealthy; literally, "flowing to"
af	fect		affect	to act on, influence, or cause change
ag	gregate		aggregate	a group of distinct things gathered into or considered as a whole (n.); to gather into a mass (v.); considered as a whole (adj.)
al	lure		allure	the quality of being tempting or charming (n.); to entice or attract (v.)
an	nex		annex	a building connected to an already existing building (n.); to add or attach (v.)

AWAY

The prefixes for away are *ab* and *apo* and may mean rejection, removal, detachment, or defense and response, as in apology.

Beginning	Root Word	Ending	New Word	Definition
ab	dicate		abdicate	to renounce or reject, as when a king gives up his throne
ab	duct		abduct	to lead astray; to take away without consent
ab	hor		abhor	to hate
apo	calypse		apocalypse	literally, to uncover; the event at the end of the world
apo	thecary		apothecary	a drug store where medicines are made or the person who makes them

MAKE A WORD

Instructions: Match the correct root word and ending together to make six words. For example, the root word "non" and the ending "agon" together make the word "nonagon." The root words and endings can be used more than once.

Root Word	Ending	New Word
ad	duct	
an	calypse	
al	gregate	
ab	vance	
ag	lure	
apo	nex	

ANALOGIES

Instructions: Using the words and definitions in this lesson, choose the best word to finish each analogy.

1. cobbler : makes shoes : : _____ : makes medicines

2. has no money : impoverished : : wealthy : _____

3. abhor : to show _____ : : adoration : to show love

4. advance : move forward : : _____ : to change habits

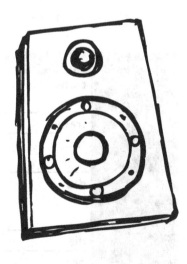

LESSON 4.6: DOWN AND THROUGH/ACROSS

CATAPULT

DOWN

Cata (Greek) and *de* (Latin through French) both mean down.

Beginning	Root Word	Ending	New Word	Definition
	de	celerate	decelerate	to slow down in speed
	de	pose	depose	to put down or remove
	de	mote	demote	to reduce in rank
	cata	strophe	catastrophe	a downturn or disaster
	cata	clysm	cataclysm	a washing down or flood

THROUGH/ACROSS

The prefixes for through and across are *tra* and *trans* (Latin), *dia* (Greek and Latin), and *per* (Latin).

Beginning	Root Word	Ending	New Word	Definition
	trans	lucent	translucent	describes a material that is semi-see-through
	trans	late	translate	to change from one language into another
	tra	dition	tradition	something handed down, as a belief or custom
	dia	meter	diameter	a line segment passing from one side to the other through the center of a circle or sphere
	dia	logue	dialogue	conversation, discussion
	per	colate	percolate	to filter through slowly
	per	spire	perspire	to sweat; to pass waste fluid through the pores of the skin

MATCHING

Instructions: Match the root words to their definitions. Definitions can be used more than once.

Root Words

1. de
2. dia
3. per
4. cata
5. trans

Definitions

a. through/across
b. down

FILL IN THE BLANK

Instructions: Use the words for Lesson 4.6 to complete the sentences below.

1. It was so hot the man started to _____ as he walked out of his house.

2. The earthquake in Haiti was a true _____, as most of the country's infrastructure was ruined.

3. During class, we read the _____ between the characters, while our teacher read the narrator's part out loud.

4. The bike flew down the hill; without the brakes, it was impossible to _____.

LESSON 4.7: AGAIN

The prefixes for again are *re* (Latin through French) and *ana* (Greek).

Beginning	Root Word	Ending	New Word	Definition
	re	tort	retort	literally, a twisting back; a sharp or quick answer in response (v.)
	re	iterate	reiterate	to say the same thing, to repeat
	re	ceptacle	receptacle	a holding back; a container
	re	taliate	retaliate	to pay back an injury or to take revenge
	re	surge	resurge	to rise again
	re	vulsion	revulsion	a violent pulling away in disgust
	re	current	recurrent	happening again and again
	ana	chronism	anachronism	a representation of something occurring at the wrong time, like a knight of old with a cell phone
	ana	gram	anagram	a rearrangement of letters in a word to make a new word

GUESS THE MEANING

Instructions: For each word below, guess its meaning, writing your guess in the second column. Then, look up the word in a dictionary and write the real meaning in the third column.

Word	I think it means . . .	It really means . . .
report		
recharge		
revise		
resign		
reconsider		
reset		
reflect		

WEB QUIZ

Instructions: Try your hand at creating words! Connect the correct root word listed in the inner circle to the word parts listed in the outer circles. You may have to use a root word more than once!

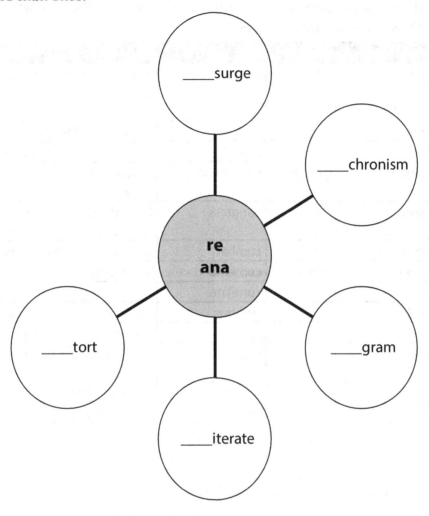

LESSON 4.8: WITH AND TOGETHER

The prefixes for with or together are *co*, *col*, *con*, *cor*, *syl*, *sym*, and *syn*. These prefixes tell you that a word deals with states of togetherness, a putting together of parts, something that occurs at the same time, and sameness.

Beginning	Root Word	Ending	New Word	Definition
	co	herent	coherent	literally, clinging together; often used to describe writing or speech that is clear and well-ordered
	co	exist	coexist	to exist together
	col	lect	collect	to gather things together
	con	gruent	congruent	coinciding, as in geometry; agreeing together
	con	gress	congress	legislative body that comes together to make laws or debate questions
	com	bat	combat	to fight with, the act of fighting
	com	bine	combine	join together
	cor	relate	correlate	to relate together
	syl	labus	syllabus	a summary or outline for a course of study
	sym	bol	symbol	something that represents another thing
	sym	pathy	sympathy	quality of having kind feelings for another's pain
	syn	chronize	synchronize	to do simultaneously
	syn	drome	syndrome	different symptoms occurring together

MATCHING

Instructions: Match the words to their definitions.

Words
1. collect
2. coexist
3. syndrome
4. combat
5. congress
6. symbol

Definitions
a. something that represents something else
b. act of fighting
c. legislative body
d. to gather together
e. to exist together
f. different symptoms occurring together

SCRAMBLER

Instructions: Unscramble each word listed below. Use the clues to help you decipher the words.

iconenrshzy
(do simultaneously)

lraceoter
(relate together)

typhamys
(to feel another's emotions)

micoben
(join together)

gerntcuon
(coinciding)

lubaslys
(outline for a course)

hercoten
(well-ordered thoughts or writing)

LESSON 4.9: WITHOUT

Prefixes and forms showing without are *il*, *im*, *in*, *ir*, *an*, *un*, *a*, and *non*.

Beginning	Root Word	Ending	New Word	Definition
il	lusion	illusion	a false idea or conception
il	literate	illiterate	not able to read
im	balanced	imbalanced	not balanced
im	perfect	imperfect	not perfect
in	sincere	insincere	not sincere
in	definite	indefinite	without limits or boundaries; not sure
ir	responsible	irresponsible	not responsible
an	onymous	anonymous	without a name; unable to be credited to any one individual
an	archy	anarchy	no rule by anyone; chaos
un	altered	unaltered	not altered or changed
un	spoken	unspoken	not spoken, silent
a	symmetrical	asymmetrical	uneven in proportion
a	typical	atypical	not typical
non	conformist	nonconformist	one who does not follow norms or customs
non	profit	nonprofit	without profit; often a charitable institution

GUESS THE MEANING

Instructions: For each word below, guess its meaning, writing your guess in the second column. Then, look up the word in a dictionary and write the real meaning in the third column.

Word	I think it means . . .	It really means . . .
incapable		
nontraditional		
unusual		
improper		
illegible		
unbelievable		
impossible		

WEB QUIZ

Instructions: Try your hand at creating words! Connect the correct root word listed in the inner circle to the word parts listed in the outer circles. You may have to use a root word more than once!

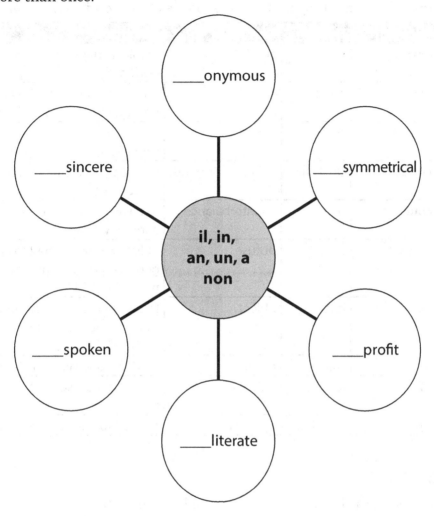

LESSON 4.10: AGAINST

Anti (Greek and Latin through French) means against, while *contra*, *counter*, and *ob*, *oc*, *of*, and *op* (Latin) signal something that is the opposite of, thick, hidden, or against.

Beginning	Root Word	Ending	New Word	Definition
	anti	dote	antidote	medicine given as a remedy against a poison
	anta	gonist	antagonist	one who challenges the hero, heroine, or protagonist in a work of fiction
	contra	st	contrast	to set side by side to determine differences; something showing differences
	counter	clockwise	counterclockwise	In an opposite direction of the clock's movement
	counter	balance	counterbalance	to balance against, or offset a weight by another weight
	ob	tuse	obtuse	dull, fat, thick; applied to angles in geometry or sometimes to people who are mentally "thick"
	ob	ject	object	to disagree, to protest; something perceived through the senses; noun that receives the action of the verb
	oc	cult	occult	hidden, concealed; the supernatural world
	of	fensive	offensive	that which causes disgust or outrage; a military campaign
	op	pression	oppression	a pressing against or keeping down forcibly

FILL IN THE BLANK
. . . .
Instructions: Use the words for Lesson 4.10 to complete the sentences below.

1. Lord Voldemort is the _____ in the *Harry Potter* series.

2. I hoped that the comedian's jokes wouldn't be _____ to anyone, but my friends all seemed to love him.

3. We had to gather in a circle, then pass the ball _____ to our teammates, the opposite of the order we expected.

4. "You are so _____ if you can't understand that I'm trying to tell you I love you," the heroine yelled as she saw the confused look on his face.

5. We wrote a letter to the principal, stating that the new uniform rule was an _____ of our personal style.

WEB QUIZ

Instructions: Try your hand at creating words! Connect the correct root word listed in the inner circle to the word parts listed in the outer circles. You may have to use a root word more than once!

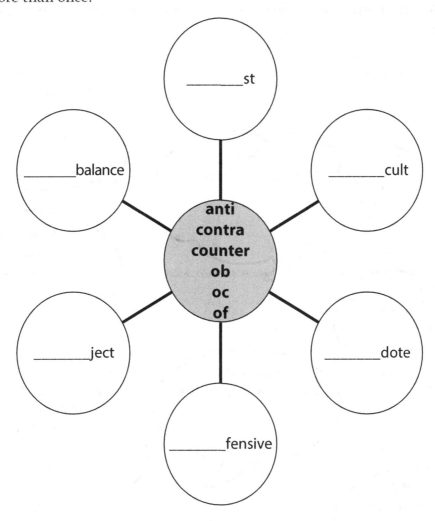

CHAPTER 4 REVIEW

WORD BUBBLES

Instructions: Add the prefixes in the word bank to the bubbles to make words that match the definitions.

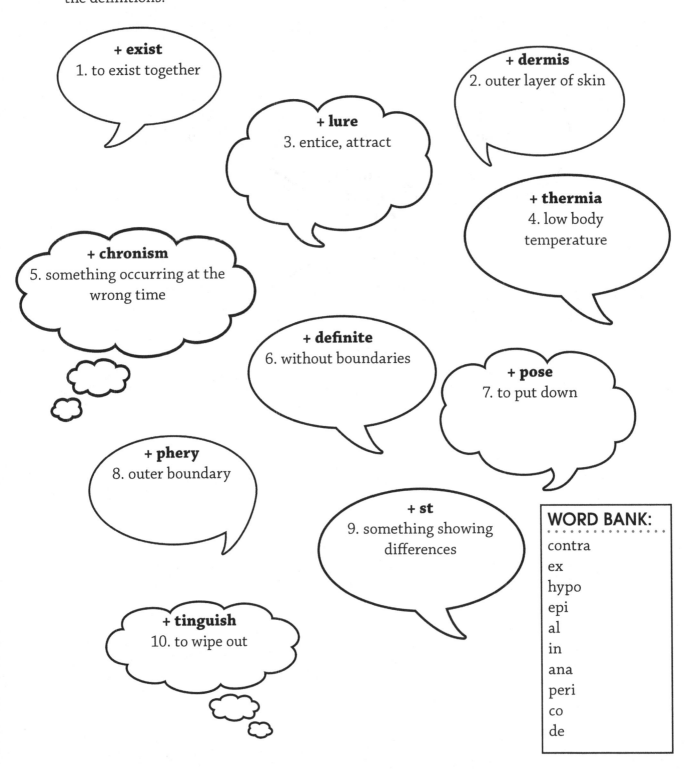

+ **exist**
1. to exist together

+ **dermis**
2. outer layer of skin

+ **lure**
3. entice, attract

+ **thermia**
4. low body temperature

+ **chronism**
5. something occurring at the wrong time

+ **definite**
6. without boundaries

+ **pose**
7. to put down

+ **phery**
8. outer boundary

+ **st**
9. something showing differences

+ **tinguish**
10. to wipe out

WORD BANK:
contra
ex
hypo
epi
al
in
ana
peri
co
de

CHAPTER 5

Shapes, Qualities, Colors

This chapter covers the many borrowed roots we use to describe shapes, and different kinds of shapes from straight, or crooked, to flat, or twisted. This chapter also covers both colors and qualities—or other ways in which we describe the objects around us.

Color makes up much of what we see in the world. With the exception of some rare people who cannot see certain colors, color makes us happy, dazzles our eyes, makes our mouths water, and helps us identify everyday objects. Do you think you'd like to eat a blue spotted banana, or perhaps green eggs? Though they might be delicious, your pushing away food like that would be understandable. Color is the way many animals, humans included, are able to decide what is safe to eat, and that's no small advantage!

When we are children, some of the first words we learn are words to describe what we want or what we see. Concepts like good and bad, same and different, hard and soft, heavy and light are ones that we sense in our infancy, even before we know the words for them.

LESSON 5.F: SHAPES

WELL, MY MOM SAYS YOU'RE A FIGMENT OF MY IMAGINATION!

The Latin roots for shape are *fig*, *fac(e)*, and *form* and indicate likeness or outer appearance.

Beginning	Root Word	Ending	New Word	Definition
	fig	ure	figure	likeness, shape, form, or number
	fig	ment	figment	fiction; something made up or imagined
con	**fig**	uration	configuration	a form or shape
sur	**face**		surface	the outside face of any object or the outward appearance of anything
	face	t	facet	a shiny side or surface of a cut gemstone
ef	**face**		efface	to rub or wipe out
de	**face**		deface	to spoil the appearance of something
de	**form**		deform	to disfigure; to put out of shape
	form	ation	formation	a shaping or thing shaped; an arrangement, as of soldiers, sports team players, aircraft, or warships
	form	less	formless	without shape or form

WEB QUIZ

Instructions: Try your hand at creating words! Connect the correct root word listed in the inner circle to the word parts listed in the outer circles. You may have to use a root word more than once!

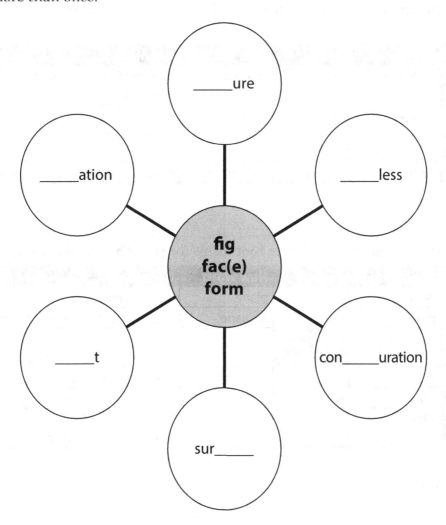

WHAT DOESN'T BELONG?

Instructions: Choose the word in each line that *does not* mean the same as the first word.

1. **figment**   fictional   imagined   real

2. **efface**   go out   wipe out   rub out

3. **deform**   disfigure   configure   put out of shape

4. **surface**   outdoors   outside face   outer appearance

5. **formation**   shaping   arrangement   surface

LESSON 5.2: STRAIGHT AND LEVEL/FLAT

STRAIGHT

Ortho (Latin through French) is used in medical terminology for the science of straightening.

Beginning	Root Word	Ending	New Word	Definition
	ortho	tics	orthotics	branch of medicine that uses braces to make limbs straighter
	ortho	pedics	orthopedics	branch of medicine treating deformities, diseases, and injuries of the bones and joints
	ortho	dontist	orthodontist	dentist that fixes uneven teeth

LEVEL/FLAT

Plan, plain (Latin), *platy*, and *plat* are root forms for smooth, straight, level, or flat.

Beginning	Root Word	Ending	New Word	Definition
	plan	e	plane	a flat, level, and even surface
air	**plan**	e	airplane	fixed-wing self-propelled aircraft
	plain		plain	large level land area (n.); simple, ordinary, common, frank, obvious, clear (adj.)
	platy	pus	platypus	small flat-footed animal native to Australia
	plat	eau	plateau	an elevated, flat, land area
	plat	form	platform	raised level surface or floor; a statement of principles for a political party

MAKE A WORD

Instructions: Match the correct root word and ending together to make five words. For example, the root word "non" and the ending "agon" together make the word "nonagon." The root words and endings can be used more than once.

Root Word	Ending	New Word
ortho	form	
plan	tics	
plat	e	
	dontist	
	eau	

CHANGE IT UP

Instructions: Replace the underlined word or words in each sentence with one of the vocabulary words in the word bank.

Word Bank: orthopedic, plain, platypus, plateau

1. Above the <u>elevated, flat land area</u> of the mountain was an isolated village.

2. She spoke in a <u>clear, obvious</u> manner, hoping to get her point across.

3. When my teammate hurt his ankle, the coach suggested he see an <u>bone and joint specialist</u> doctor.

4. My favorite exhibit was home to the <u>flat-footed animal</u> from Australia.

Name:_____ Date:_____

LESSON 5.3: COLOR

Chrom comes from Greek to mean color.

Beginning	Root Word	Ending	New Word	Definition
	chrom	e	chrome	brightly colored metallic alloy used for plating
	chrom	atic	chromatic	having color or brightly colored
mono	**chrom**	atic	monochromatic	having only one color or color scheme (such as shades of blue)
poly	**chrom**	atic	polychromatic	showing a range or variety of colors; multicolored
	chrom	ium	chromium	an element so named because it makes brilliantly colored compounds
	chrom	osome	chromosome	colored, rod-shaped bodies in the nucleus of cells

WORD SPLITS

Instructions: The makers of a new dictionary want to break up some words into their word parts for their new edition, but need your help! Can you divide the following words into their word parts? Think carefully—a few words may be new to you!

1. chrome: _____ + _____

2. chromosome: _____ + _____

3. polychromatic: _____ + _____ + _____

4. chromatology: _____ + _____

5. chromatist: _____ + _____

Rockin' Root Words Book 2 © Taylor & Francis Group • Permission is granted to photocopy or reproduce this page for single classroom use only.

WORD MATH

Instructions: Read the instructions in the box in order to create a new word by changing the word before it. Use the clues at the bottom of the box to help you create the new words.

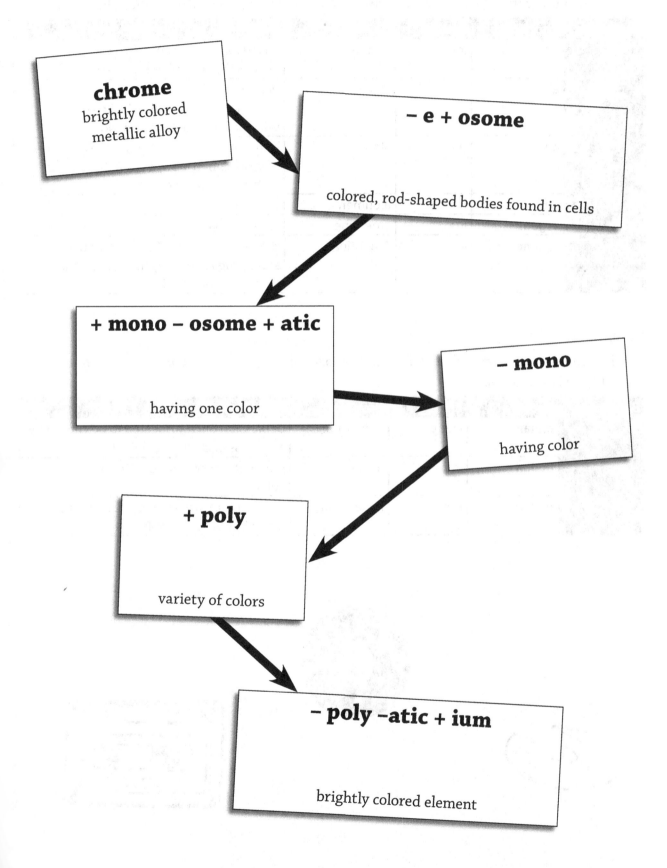

chrome
brightly colored metallic alloy

– e + osome
colored, rod-shaped bodies found in cells

+ mono – osome + atic
having one color

– mono
having color

+ poly
variety of colors

– poly –atic + ium
brightly colored element

LESSON 5.4: WHITE/SILVER AND BLACK

WHITE/SILVER

Two forms signifying white or silver are *alb* (Latin) and *argent* (Latin through French).

Beginning	Root Word	Ending	New Word	Definition
	alb	ion	Albion	an old name for England, so called after the white cliffs on the English coast
	alb	inism	albinism	genetic condition in humans and animals showing an abnormal lack of color in the skin and hair due to lack of pigment
	alb	um	album	roman writing tablet where public notices were inscribed; now, it is a notebook for pictures or drawings
	alb	umen	albumen	white of the egg
	argent	ine	argentine	silver or silvery
	argent	ina	Argentina	the "Silver Republic," named for the silver jewelry worn by the natives during European colonization

BLACK

The root for black comes from Greek in the form of *melan*, which takes on additional connotations of sadness.

Beginning	Root Word	Ending	New Word	Definition
	melan	choly	melancholy	depression once suspected to be caused by an excess of black bile in the body
	melan	in	melanin	pigment responsible for skin, eye, and hair color
	melan	oma	melanoma	a black pigmented skin cancer derived from melanin-producing cells

WEB QUIZ

Instructions: Try your hand at creating words! Connect the correct root word listed in the inner circle to the word parts listed in the outer circles. You may have to use a root word more than once!

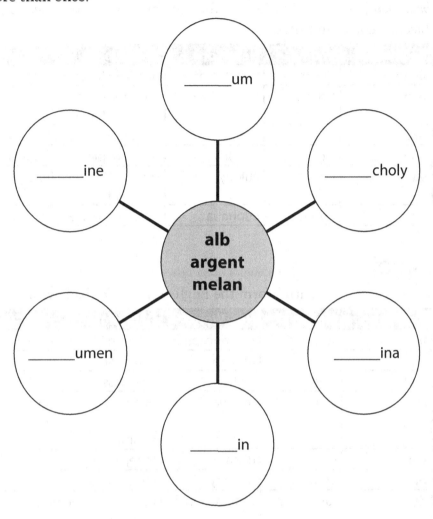

FILL IN THE BLANK

Instructions: Use the words for Lesson 5.4 to complete the sentences below.

1. Many people from the sub-Saharan desert region have a pigment called

   _____ in their skin to withstand the heat from the sun's rays.

2. The teacup pig I picked out at the pet store suffered from _____;

   everything on him was lightly colored, including his eyelashes.

3. Juan, Cara, Desrick, and I chose to do our social studies class project on

   _____, the Silver Republic.

4. The eliminated singer looked so _____ as she sang her

   farewell song on my favorite reality TV show.

LESSON 5.5: GOOD/WELL AND BAD/WRONG

GOOD/WELL

The roots *bene*, *bon* (Latin), and *eu* (Greek) find homes in words that describe the relative goodness of objects, people, and situations.

Beginning	Root Word	Ending	New Word	Definition
	bene	factor	benefactor	one who helps others
	bene	volence	benevolence	"good wishing"; action to promote the welfare of others
	bon	us	bonus	a prize or unexpected reward
de	bon	air	debonair	suave, of pleasant manner, genial
	eu	logy	eulogy	speech given at a funeral; speaking well of the dead
	eu	phoria	euphoria	giddy elation, ecstatic joy

BAD/WRONG/NOT

Mis, *mal(e)*, *dis*, *dys*, and *dif* (Latin) form the English words for bad, wrong, and not.

Beginning	Root Word	Ending	New Word	Definition
	mis	conception	misconception	a wrong idea or view of something
	mis	hap	mishap	a mistake, blunder, or accident
	mal	ady	malady	an illness
	mal	aria	malaria	disease spread by infected mosquitoes, once believed to be caused by the bad air in swamps
	dis	card	discard	to reject or get rid of
	dis	array	disarray	chaos, disorder
	dys	functional	dysfunctional	not functioning properly, impaired, abnormal
	dif	fuse	diffuse	to spread out in area (v.); not concentrated; spread out (adj.)

MATCHING

Instructions: Match the root words to their definitions. Definitions can be used more than once.

Root Words
1. bene
2. dis
3. dif
4. bon
5. eu
6. mal

Definitions
a. good
b. bad

Rockin' Root Words Book 2 © Taylor & Francis Group • Permission is granted to photocopy or reproduce this page for single classroom use only.

THINKING ABOUT VOCABULARY

Instructions: When we use the word *disaster*, we are actually drawing on the ancient belief that says that stars (*aster*) determine a person's future. Use the vocabulary in this lesson to answer the following questions.

1. What is it called when someone doesn't understand a particular viewpoint?

   _____

2. If you were to work hard and get a lot accomplished in your job, what might you receive?

   _____

3. A eulogy is a speech that celebrates the life of someone who has died. Pick a famous person from history and write a five line poem that could have been used as a eulogy at his or her funeral.

   _____

   _____

   _____

   _____

   _____

4. Natural disasters affect people on a regular basis around the world, regardless of where they live and what they have. Such disasters can change everything in an instant. Pretend you are collecting items for donation to victims of a recent natural disaster. On another piece of paper, draw a flyer asking for donations. Your flyer should include information about the disaster, its victims, and what they need in order to recover. Use at least one of your vocabulary words from this lesson in your flyer.

LESSON 5.6: SAME/ALMOST THE SAME

The Greek root for sameness is *homo*; the Latin root is *simul*. Another root for sameness is *sembl*.

Beginning	Root Word	Ending	New Word	Definition
	homo	genize	homogenize	to make uniform in consistency, as milk
	homo	nym	homonym	words that sound alike and are spelled alike, but have different meanings (e.g., left and left)
	simil	ar	similar	state of being like another thing
	simil	e	simile	a literary term featuring a stated comparison
as	**simil**	ate	assimilate	to make similar; to integrate a part into a whole
	simul	ator	simulator	a testing device to create conditions in a lab similar to real conditions
	simul	taneous	simultaneous	at the same time
as	**sembl**	e	assemble	to put together
en	**sembl**	e	ensemble	a group of actors, dancers, or musicians who perform together
re	**sembl**	ance	resemblance	quality of resembling or likeness

WORD SPLITS

Instructions: The makers of a new dictionary want to break up some words into their word parts for their new edition, but need your help! Can you divide the following words into their word parts? Think carefully—a few words may be new to you!

1. homonym: _____ + _____

2. simile: _____ + _____

3. resemble: _____ + _____ + _____

4. assimilate: _____ + _____ + _____

5. assembly: _____ + _____ + _____

ALL MIXED UP

Instructions: Help! The following word parts were all mixed up in the dictionary. Connect the word parts by drawing lines between the boxes. Then, write the correct words in the lines next to their definitions. Be careful! Some of the connections can be tricky: You only want to find words that match the definitions below.

1. _____: group that performs together

2. _____: at the same time

3. _____: being like another thing

4. _____: to make uniform

5. _____: testing device

6. _____: to put together

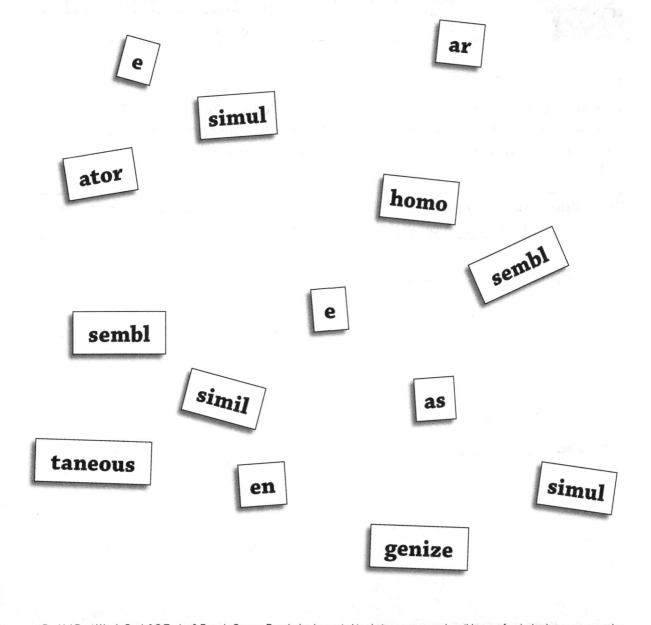

LESSON 5.7: DIFFERENT/OTHER

The roots used to portray different qualities or contrasts are *hetero* (Greek), *ali/all/alle* (Latin), and *vari* (Latin).

Beginning	Root Word	Ending	New Word	Definition
	hetero	geneous	heterogeneous	of different kinds
	ali	as	alias	a different name that one goes by; pseudonym
	ali	en	alien	stranger or foreigner (n.); strange (adj.)
	ali	enate	alienate	to cause to be isolated, withdrawn, or detached
	all	ergy	allergy	a hypersensitivity to a specific substance
	alle	gory	allegory	a story that has a second, symbolic meaning
	vari	ant	variant	varying, different from others of the same kind or class
	vari	able	variable	changeable (adj.); anything changeable (n.)
	vari	ation	variation	the act of changing forms or providing diversity

SYNONYM SEARCH

Instructions: Sort through the words in the word bank to find synonyms for the vocabulary words listed below. Write the synonyms on the lines next to the words they correspond with. Be careful—some of the words in the word bank will not be used!

Word Bank: pseudonym, isolated, changeable, citizen, hypersensitivity, changing forms, foreigner, different kinds, meaningful story, witness

1. allegory _____

2. alien _____

3. heterogeneous _____

4. alias _____

5. variable _____

6. allergy _____

WEB QUIZ

Instructions: Try your hand at creating words! Connect the correct root word listed in the inner circle to the word parts listed in the outer circles. You may have to use a root word more than once!

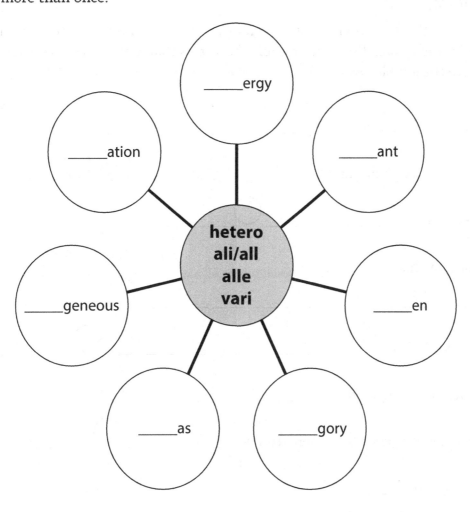

CHAPTER 5 REVIEW

WORD JUMBLE

Instructions: Use the definitions below and your word tables in this chapter to fill in the blanks for each word. Then, unscramble the letters that appear in circles to find the answer to the jumbled word!

1. Depression, sadness   ___ ___ ___ ___ ___ ___ ___ ___ (○)

2. To cause to be withdrawn   ___ ___ ___ ___ ___ ___ (○) ___

3. Spread out   ___ ___ ___ ___ (○) ___ ___

4. A form or shape
   ___ ___ ___ (○) ___ ___ ___ ___ ___ (○) ___ ___

5. To make part of a whole   ___ ___ ___ ___ ___ ___ (○) ___ ___

6. Old name for England   ___ ___ ___ ___ ___ (○)

7. To spoil the appearance of something   ___ ___ ___ (○) ___ ___

8. Having color   ___ ___ ___ ___ ___ ___ ___ (○)

9. Treatment that uses braces to straighten limbs
   ___ ___ ___ ___ (○) ___ ___ ___ (○)

10. Suave, genial   (○) ___ ___ ___ (○) ___ ___ ___

Jumbled Word: Not functioning, impaired, abnormal

___ ___ ___ ___ ___ ___ ___ ___ ___ ___ ___ ___ ___

CHAPTER 6

Bodily Structures

For its time, Greek medicine was the most advanced in the world. Although many of their medical theories have been proven false, the Greek's attention to detail, and careful observations set the standard for medical practice for hundreds of years. The Romans learned from the Greeks and, as a result, much of the terminology they used (and passed on to us indirectly through loaned words) has become part of our medical vocabulary.

LESSON 6.1: ORGANS AND HEART

ORGANS

Organ derives from Greek and Latin and has come to mean not only organ, but also a system.

Beginning	Root Word	Ending	New Word	Definition
	organ		organ	specialized tissue in the body that performs a specific function; a musical instrument
	organ	elles	organelles	tiny structures or organs within bodily cells
	organ	ism	organism	living animal, plant, bacterium
dis	**organ**	ized	disorganized	not organized
micro	**organ**	ism	microorganism	tiny organism (e.g., bacterium)

HEART

The roots *card* (Greek), *cord* (Latin), and *cour* (French) all mean heart. These roots pertain to not only the actual organ, but also emotions of the heart.

Beginning	Root Word	Ending	New Word	Definition
	card	iac	cardiac	pertaining to the heart
ac	**cord**		accord	harmony or agreement between persons (n.); to agree (v.)
dis	**cord**		discord	disagreement; lack of harmony
con	**cord**		concord	agreement
re	**cord**		record	to call to mind, preserve the evidence for, or remember (v.); literally, to bring back to the heart
	cour	age	courage	bravery, fearlessness, valor
en	**cour**	age	encourage	to give heart or boost in confidence
en	**cour**	agement	encouragement	act of encouraging or boosting

WEB QUIZ

Instructions: Try your hand at creating words! Connect the correct root word listed in the inner circle to the word parts listed in the outer circles. You may have to use a root word more than once!

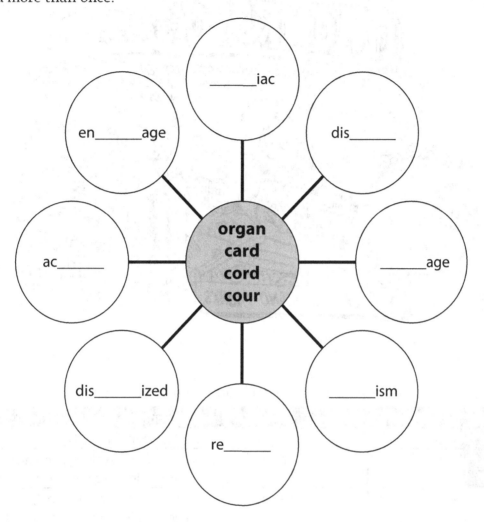

PICK THE WORD

Instructions: Choose the best word or phrase that completes each sentence.

1. The lion in *The Wizard of Oz* was so afraid and lacked the (*concord, encourage, courage*) to do anything alone.

2. After hearing Kaleb's story, I encouraged my parents to become (*organelle, organ, microorganism*) donors.

3. There was a lot of (*discord, accord, concord*) in the group; no one would choose a movie.

4. I tried to (*record, courage, encourage*) my best friend to study harder for the math test.

LESSON 6.2: HEAD AND TEETH

HEAD

Cap/capt/capit comes from Latin to mean head or top of the body.

Beginning	Root Word	Ending	New Word	Definition
	cap	a	capa	red cloak of a bullfighter
	cap	e	cape	hooded sleeveless garment; piece of land projecting into the sea, headland
es	**cap**	e	escape	literally, "out of the cape"; breaking out or getting free; an avoidance of something
	cap	puccino	cappuccino	brown hood worn by certain monks; a coffee drink topped with foamy milk
	capt	ain	captain	leader or head of a group; military rank
	capit	al	capital	accumulated investment money (n.); serious, chief (adj.)
	capit	ol	capitol	the seat of a government

TEETH

The Latin roots for teeth are *dent* and *dont* and describe anything with pointed "teeth."

Beginning	Root Word	Ending	New Word	Definition
	dent	ist	dentist	tooth care specialist
	dent	ure	denture	artificial set of teeth
in	**dent**		indent	to make a dent or notch into
ortho	**dont**	ist	orthodontist	a dental specialist who straightens teeth with braces

MATCHING

Instructions: Match the root words to their definitions. Definitions can be used more than once.

Root Words

1. dent
2. cap
3. dont

Definitions

a. head
b. teeth

ANALOGIES

Instructions: Using the words and definitions in this lesson, choose the best word to finish each analogy.

1. orthopedic surgeon : straightens bones : : _____ : straightens teeth

2. _____ : army : : president : country

3. cupcake : dessert : : cappuccino : _____

4. goalie : pads : : _____ : capa

LESSON 6.3: HANDS

The root words for hands are *man(u)* (Latin), *chiro* (Greek), *dexter*, and *cap* (Latin). These roots signify having, holding, taking, and seizing. Be careful not to mistake *cap* meaning hands for *cap* meaning head.

Beginning	Root Word	Ending	New Word	Definition
	manu	facture	manufacture	to make by hand; now, to produce by machinery in a factory
	man(u)	icurist	manicurist	person who cares for hands and nails
	man(u)	euver	maneuver	a strategic or tactical movement of troops or war vehicles in war or simulated war; any attempt at skillful or successful movement
e	man(u)	cipate	emancipate	to release or free someone from bondage
	man(u)	date	mandate	to order, command
	man(u)	ner	manner	way of acting or doing; characteristic style
	chiro	practor	chiropractor	person who uses manipulation of bone joints, especially the spine, as a medical treatment
	dexter	ity	dexterity	skill in using hands or body; grace
	cap	tion	caption	explanation for a picture or an illustration
	cap	ture	capture	to take by force (v.); the taking by force, seizure (n.)
	cap	acity	capacity	ability to take in or contain; potential, power

WHAT DOESN'T BELONG?

Instructions: Choose the word in each line that *does not* mean the same as the first word.

1. **mandate**   order   ask   command

2. **capture**   take   seize   release

3. **dexterity**   skill using hands   talking a lot   able to move with grace

4. **emancipate**   capture   release   free

5. **capacity**   potential   power   inability

WEB QUIZ

Instructions: Try your hand at creating words! Connect the correct root word listed in the inner circle to the word parts listed in the outer circles. You may have to use a root word more than once!

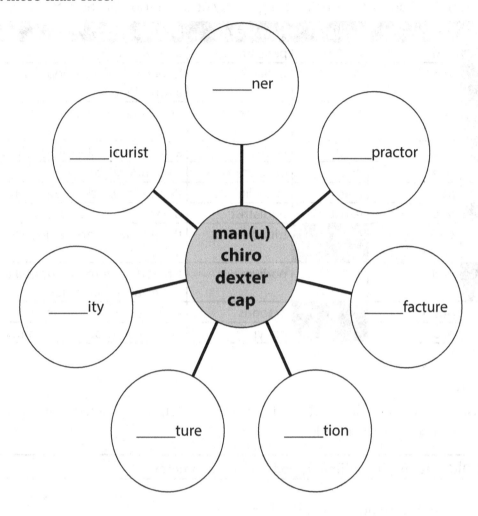

LESSON 6.4: Feet

Root words for feet are *ped* (Latin through French), *pod* (Greek), and *pus* (Greek). These roots appear in English to describe walking or any other motion of the feet.

Beginning	Root Word	Ending	New Word	Definition
	ped	estrian	pedestrian	one who walks
	ped	al	pedal	lever or pad for the foot that causes motion, as on a bicycle
	ped	ometer	pedometer	instrument to measure distance traveled on foot
	ped	estal	pedestal	a foot or base of a pillar; column-like stand
ex	**ped**	ition	expedition	a journey or voyage
im	**ped**	iment	impediment	that which blocks progress; hindrance
	pod	iatrist	podiatrist	doctor who cares for feet
tri	**pod**		tripod	three-footed stand, as in a stool; support for a camera
	pod	ium	podium	a raised platform or low wall that serves as a pedestal or foundation
octo	**pus**		octopus	eight-footed marine animal
platy	**pus**		platypus	flat-footed Australian mammal

CHANGE IT UP

Instructions: Replace the underlined word or words in each sentence with one of the vocabulary words in the word bank.

Word Bank: octopus, impediment, podiatrist, pedometer

1. Our semester health project required us to wear a <u>instrument used to measure distance</u> for a week to see how far we had walked.
2. The pain in my flat feet grew so bad that I finally had to consult a <u>foot doctor</u>.
3. We watched with amazement as the <u>eight-footed creature</u> moved from one rock to another in the aquarium.
4. His declaration that he really despised romantic comedies was an <u>hindrance</u> to my plans to see the newest movie.

WORD MATH

Instructions: Read the instructions in the box in order to create a new word by changing the word before it. Use the clues at the bottom of the box to help you create the new words.

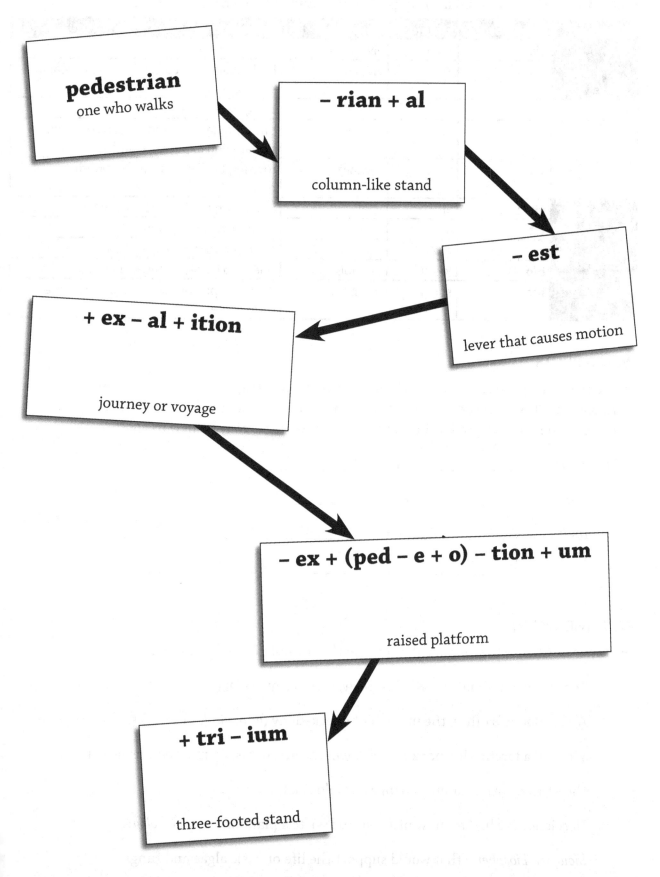

pedestrian
one who walks

– rian + al

column-like stand

– est

lever that causes motion

+ ex – al + ition

journey or voyage

– ex + (ped – e + o) – tion + um

raised platform

+ tri – ium

three-footed stand

LESSON 6.5: Life

The roots for life are *viv* (Latin), *vit* (Latin), *zo* (Greek), and *bio* (Greek and Latin). These roots take on the additional meanings of vitality and of being necessary for life.

Beginning	Root Word	Ending	New Word	Definition
	viv	acious	vivacious	lively, attractive
	viv	id	vivid	lively, animated, colorful, forming clear or striking images
re	**viv**	e	revive	bring back to life again
sur	**viv**	or	survivor	one who has endured hardship or a life-threatening experience and lived
re	**vit**	alize	revitalize	to bring back energy and strength; to rejuvenate
	vit	al	vital	belonging to life or necessary for life
	vit	a	vita	a life-history or resume
	zo	ology	zoology	science and study of animals
	bio	logist	biologist	one who studies living organisms
	bio	sphere	biosphere	area on a planet that can support some form of life

WORD SPLITS

Instructions: The makers of a new dictionary want to break up some words into their word parts for their new edition, but need your help! Can you divide the following words into their word parts? Think carefully—a few words may be new to you!

1. vivacity: _____ + _____

2. zodiac: _____ + _____

3. revitalize: _____ + _____ + _____

4. revival: _____ + _____ + _____

PICK THE WORD

Instructions: Choose the best word or phrase that completes each sentence.

1. The study of animals is called (*biology, psychology, zoology*).

2. At the doctor's office, the nurse first checked my (*vita, vital, survivor*) signs.

3. We read a fascinating book called *Night*, about a (*survivor, vivacious, revive*) of

   the concentration camps during the Holocaust.

4. In science, we had to draw pictures and write a plan for a mini (*zoology,*

   biologist, biosphere) that would support the life of basic algae and fungi.

Name:_____ Date:_____

LESSON 6.6: END/BOUNDARY AND DEATH

END/BOUNDARY

The Latin roots for end are *fin*, *term*, and *lim*.

Beginning	Root Word	Ending	New Word	Definition
	fin	ale	finale	the last part of a production that has a great impact
	fin	ite	finite	having measurable limits
in	fin	ite	infinite	lacking limits or boundaries, endless, vast
	term	inal	terminal	at, or forming the end of something (adj.); a station on a transportation line (n.); a connective device in an electrical circuit (n.)
	term	inate	terminate	to come to an end
	lim	it	limit	boundary, point where something ends
e	lim	inate	eliminate	literally, to put out of doors; to reject, remove, or drop from consideration

DEATH

Mort (Latin) and *thana* (Greek) are roots meaning the end, death, or the process of dying.

Beginning	Root Word	Ending	New Word	Definition
	mort	al	mortal	a human being; causing death
im	mort	al	immortal	living forever; deathless
	mort	ician	mortician	a funeral director
eu	thana	sia	euthanasia	mercy-killing; causing death to end suffering

FILL IN THE BLANK

Instructions: Use the words for Lesson 6.6 to complete the sentences below.

1. Someone who is _____ will inevitably die.

2. I had to _____ my contract with my cell phone carrier

   because their rates were so high.

3. From the mountain top, the view seemed to be _____, going

   on forever.

4. She wanted to _____ the last contestant, but the remaining

   judges convinced her otherwise.

WEB QUIZ

Instructions: Try your hand at creating words! Connect the correct root word listed in the inner circle to the word parts listed in the outer circles. You may have to use a root word more than once!

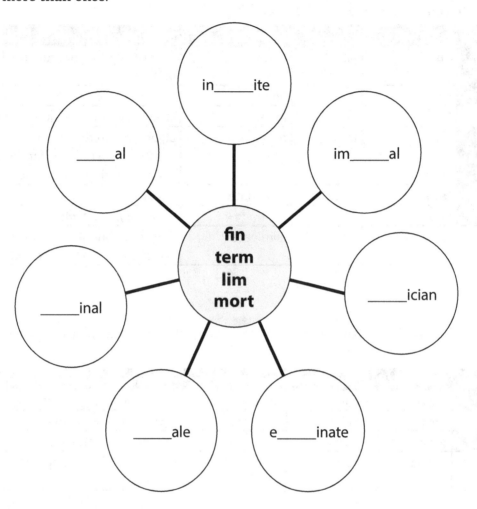

Rockin' Root Words Book 2 © Taylor & Francis Group • Permission is granted to photocopy or reproduce this page for single classroom use only.

LESSON 6.7: BODY/FLESH

THE SARCASTIC SARCOPHAGUS

The roots for body and blood are *necro* (Greek and Latin), *carn* (Latin), *corp* (Latin through French), and *sarc* (Latin through French). These roots find their home in the English words for flesh and many of the words with these roots carry connotations of death or decay.

Beginning	Root Word	Ending	New Word	Definition
	necro	polis	necropolis	cemetery, especially in an ancient city
	carn	ation	carnation	flower once considered flesh colored
	carn	ivore	carnivore	flesh-eating animal
rein	**carn**	ation	reincarnation	rebirth of the soul in another body, as in Hindu belief
	corp	oration	corporation	a governing body or chartered business firm
	corp	se	corpse	dead body
	corp	s	corps	organized body of people, such as an army unit
	sarc	oma	sarcoma	cancerous, fleshy tumor
	sarc	ophagus	sarcophagus	limestone coffin or tomb
	sarc	astic	sarcastic	having a piercing, caustic nature of mockery

MATCHING

Instructions: Match the words to their definitions.

Words	Definitions
1. carnation	a. cemetery in an ancient city
2. necropolis	b. organized body of people
3. sarcoma	c. flower considered flesh colored
4. corps	d. cancerous tumor

THINKING ABOUT VOCABULARY

The word *carnival* comes from the Latin for meat and flesh, and both were much in evidence at ancient Roman festivals. In several cities across the world, people have huge parades, parties, and general merry-making on the Tuesday prior to the time of self-denial called Lent, called *Carnivale*.

Instructions: Use the vocabulary in this lesson to answer the following questions.

1. An herbivore eats only plants. A carnivore eats mainly meat. Using your dictionary or the Internet, find the term for an animal that eats both vegetation and meat.

   _____

2. What is the name for a governing body or business firm?

   _____

3. If someone answers you with mockery in speech, you might describe their tone of voice as . . .

   _____

4. With the permission of your parents or teachers, find three countries other than Italy and the United States that host mass carnival parades or Carnivale. What countries did you find? Name one traditional element of each country's carnival.

   _____

   _____

   _____

CHAPTER 6 REVIEW

CREATE A COMIC

Instructions: What if you thought you were immortal and could never die, but one day everything changed and your life was suddenly in danger? Using your words for this chapter and the grids below, draw a comic strip about a superhero or other character who finds out he or she is suddenly mortal. What will he or she have to do to get back his or her immortality? You must use at least seven of the words found in this chapter in your comic strip.

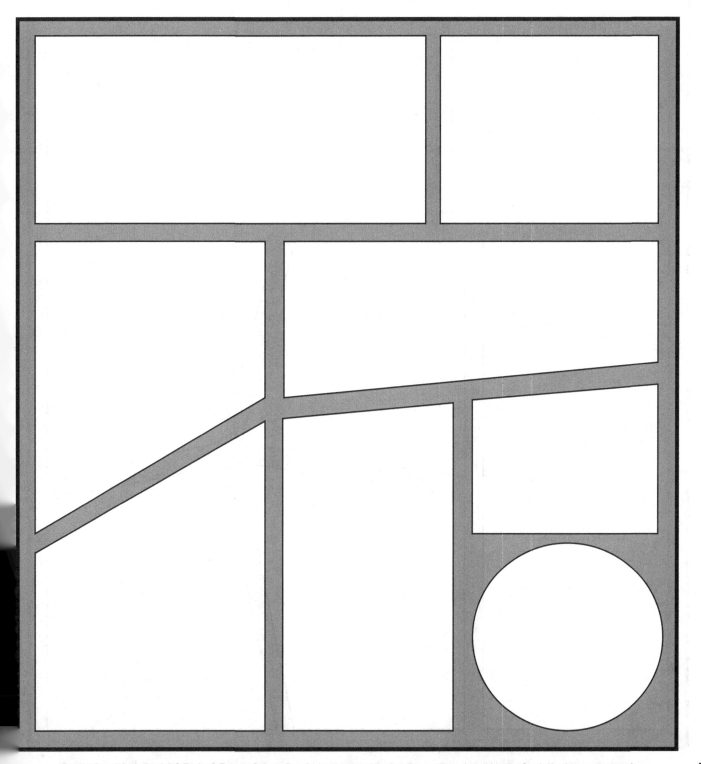

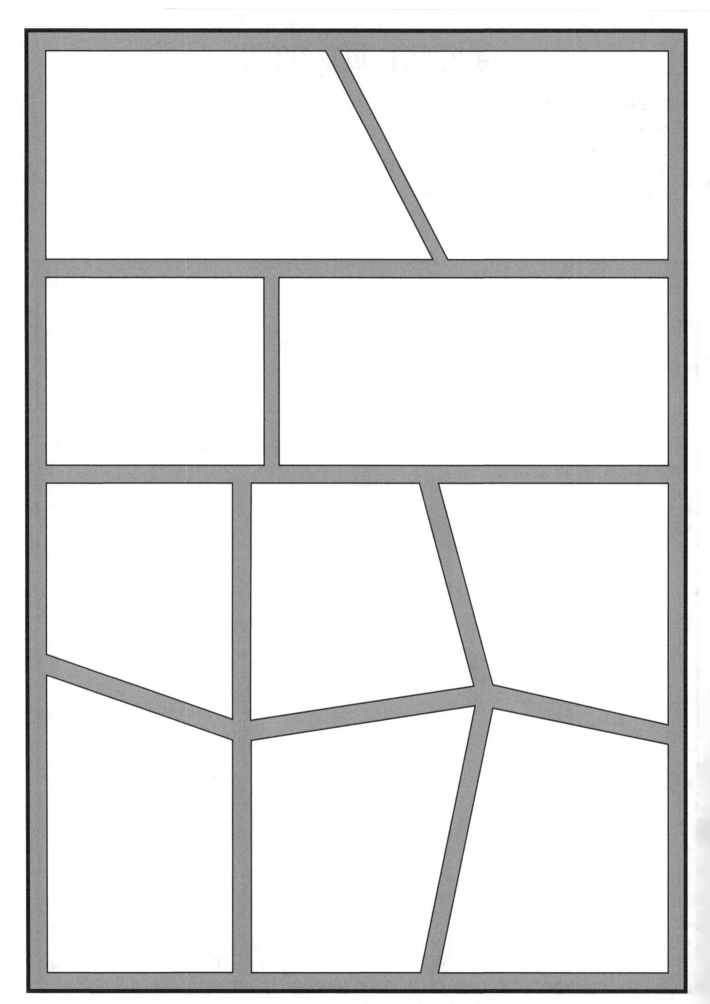

Rockin' Root Words Book 2 © Taylor & Francis Group • Permission is granted to photocopy or reproduce this page for single classroom use only.

CHAPTER 7

Bodily Senses and Emotions

The five senses are among the few *native* English words that we use every day. Smell comes from the Old English *smyllan*; taste comes from the Middle English *tasten*; hear comes from the Old English *hieren*; touch comes from the Middle English *touchen*; and see comes from the Old English *seon*. Words for objects or concepts that are physically closest to us, or that have to do directly with our personal being, tend to stay our own in origin. Why is that? If English is so willing to adopt or borrow foreign words, such as those for medicine, why do certain categories of words remain our own after hundreds of years of mixing with foreign languages?

LESSON 7.F: SEEING AND LOOKING

Vi, vis, vid, and *spec* (Latin) and *scop* (Latin and Greek) lend themselves to words pertaining to sight, to examining closely, and to what is obvious.

Beginning	Root Word	Ending	New Word	Definition
e	**vid**	ent	evident	plain, clear, obvious
pro	**vid**	e	provide	to supply, prepare for, or make a condition
	vis	age	visage	the face and its features
re	**vis**	e	revise	to look over again; to correct
super	**vis**	or	supervisor	someone who oversees
	spec	tacle	spectacle	a display for the public to see, a show
	spec	tacles	spectacles	eyeglasses, corrective lenses
in	**spec**	t	inspect	to look into or make a close examination of
micro	**scop**	e	microscope	instrument for magnifying small objects for examination
stetho	**scop**	e	stethoscope	device for medically examining the heart, lungs, and organs by listening

PICK THE WORD
. . . .
Instructions: Choose the best word or phrase that completes each sentence.

1. We had to *(inspect, visage, revise)* our papers before handing them in, fixing
   any mistakes and adding new information.

2. The doctor checked my lungs with a *(microscope, stethoscope, spectacle)* before
   diagnosing me with bronchitis.

3. Jaime's dangerous tricks on the new skateboard park's half-pipe created quite
   a *(spectacle, spectacles, visage)*, filling the park with onlookers.

4. The answer was evident to me, yet she couldn't see it, despite the fact that it
   was so *(unclear, correct, obvious)*.

WEB QUIZ

Instructions: Try your hand at creating words! Connect the correct root word listed in the inner circle to the word parts listed in the outer circles. You may have to use a root word more than once!

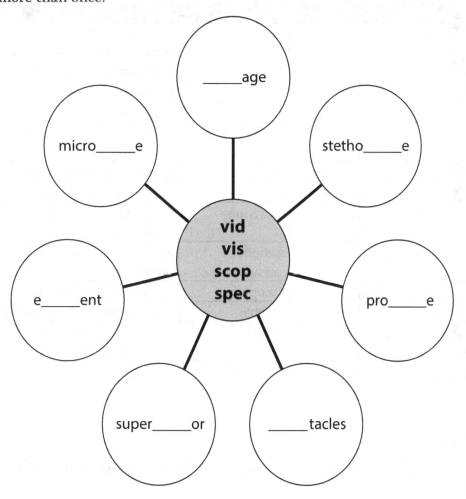

LESSON 7.2: HEARING AND SOUND

The roots for hearing and sound are *ton* (Latin), *son*, *phon* (Greek), and *aud* (Latin).

Beginning	Root Word	Ending	New Word	Definition
	ton	e	tone	a distinct musical or vocal sound; a style, trend, or atmosphere; the quality of color; a voice quality indicating mood or emotion
	ton	al	tonal	pertaining to tone or tonality
mono	**ton**	e	monotone	uninterrupted repetition of the same tone
con	**son**	ant	consonant	a letter other than a vowel (n.); in agreement or harmony (adj.)
	son	ogram	sonogram	record of an ultrasound test of a body part
	son	ic	sonic	of sound or the speed of sound
xylo	**phon**	e	xylophone	"wood sound"; a musical percussion instrument
sym	**phon**	y	symphony	an orchestra; a musical composition for an orchestra
caco	**phon**	y	cacophony	noisy or unpleasant sounds
	aud	ible	audible	of something that can be heard
	aud	ition	audition	a hearing or performance to test a candidate's fitness for a job
	aud	iovisual	audiovisual	sounds and sights recorded together in the same presentation

ANALOGIES

Instructions: Using the words and definitions in this lesson, choose the best word to finish each analogy.

1. visual : can be seen : : _____ : can be heard

2. _____ : mood or emotion : : setting : place and time

3. symphony : pleasant : : cacophony : _____

4. flute : woodwind instrument : : xylophone : _____ instrument

WEB QUIZ

Instructions: Try your hand at creating words! Connect the correct root word listed in the inner circle to the word parts listed in the outer circles. You may have to use a root word more than once!

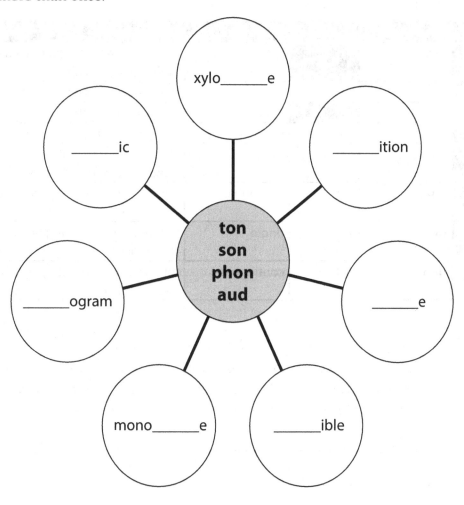

LESSON 7.3: TOUCH

The roots for touch are *tact*, *tang*, and *ting*. These roots also mean the concept of briefly touching on a subject.

Beginning	Root Word	Ending	New Word	Definition
	tact		tact	perceptive and delicate handling; poise, diplomacy, sensitivity
	tact	ile	tactile	that which can be felt by touching
in	tact		intact	whole or untouched
	tang	ible	tangible	that which can be touched; definite, clear
	tang	ent	tangent	touching, but not intersecting; off the main point; a trigonometry ratio
	tang	ential	tangential	describing wandering from the main topic or subject or merely touching on it
	ting	le	tingle	to feel a pricking, stinging, or thrilling sensation
con	ting	ent	contingent	touching or happening by chance; describing what may or may not happen

WORD SPLITS
. . . .

Instructions: The makers of a new dictionary want to break up some words into their word parts for their new edition, but need your help! Can you divide the following words into their word parts? Think carefully—a few words may be new to you!

1. intact: _____ + _____

2. tactful: _____ + _____

3. contingent: _____ + _____ + _____

4. tactile: _____ + _____

5. intangible: _____ + _____ + _____

WORD MATH

Instructions: Read the instructions in the box in order to create a new word by changing the word before it. Use the clues at the bottom of the box to help you create the new words.

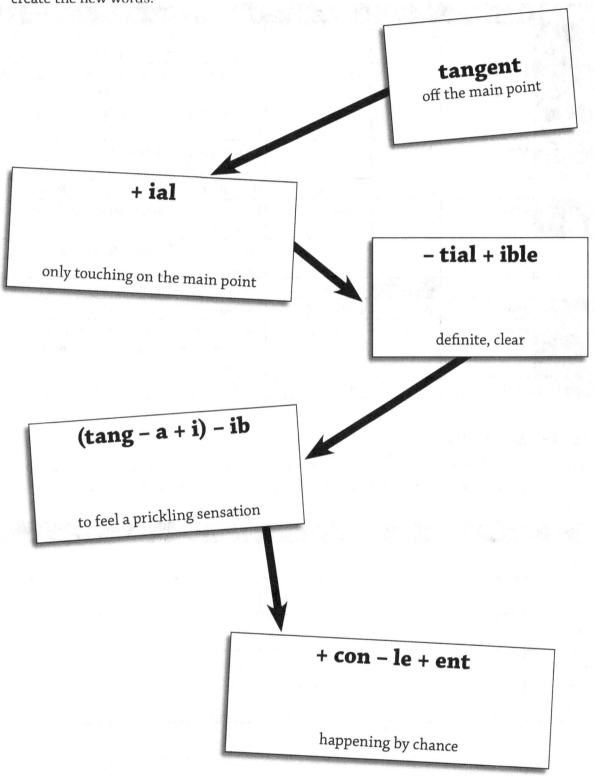

tangent
off the main point

+ ial

only touching on the main point

– tial + ible

definite, clear

(tang – a + i) – ib

to feel a prickling sensation

+ con – le + ent

happening by chance

LESSON 7.4: FEELING

Two roots for feeling are *sens* and *sent*.

Beginning	Root Word	Ending	New Word	Definition
	sens	or	sensor	device that detects and measures physical changes in the environment
	sens	e	sense	the ability of an organism to experience and react to developments in its environment; feeling, impression; something wise or reasonable
	sens	ible	sensible	showing a good quality of judgment or reason
non	**sens**	e	nonsense	that which does not make sense; foolishness
	sens	itive	sensitive	having highly tuned senses; emotionally sympathetic
in	**sens**	itive	insensitive	slow to notice, feel, or respect others' feelings
dis	**sent**		dissent	disagreement with prevailing opinion
	sent	iment	sentiment	feeling or opinion
	sent	imental	sentimental	having tender, delicate feelings; influenced by emotion (sometimes to an excessive degree)
	sent	inel	sentinel	armed guard who keeps watch

GUESS THE MEANING

Instructions: For each word below, guess its meaning, writing your guess in the second column. Then, look up the word in a dictionary and write the real meaning in the third column.

Word	I think it means . . .	It really means . . .
insensible		
sensory		
senseless		
sensational		
consent		

WEB QUIZ

Instructions: Try your hand at creating words! Connect the correct root word listed in the inner circle to the word parts listed in the outer circles. You may have to use a root word more than once!

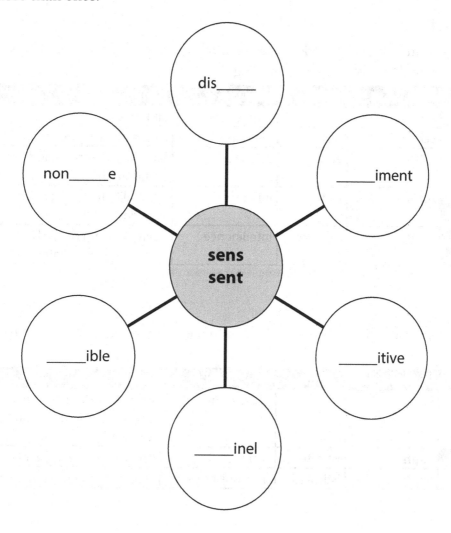

LESSON 7.5: KNOWLEDGE, WISDOM, AND MEMORY

KNOWLEDGE

Sci comes from Latin to mean knowledge. *Intel* comes from Latin and forms the foundation for English words about knowing.

Beginning	Root Word	Ending	New Word	Definition
omni	**sci**	ent	omniscient	all-knowing
con	**sci**	ous	conscious	aware, thinking, feeling, waking
con	**sci**	ence	conscience	knowledge of right and wrong; moral sense or judgment
	intel	lect	intellect	the ability to reason or understand; a superior mind
	intel	ligence	intelligence	ability to learn or apply knowledge; a measure of one's intellect

WISDOM

The root *soph* comes from Greek and Latin to mean possession of or the pursuit of wisdom.

Beginning	Root Word	Ending	New Word	Definition
philo	**soph**	y	philosophy	love of wisdom; a branch of learning treating the issues of human existence and knowledge
	soph	isticate	sophisticate	one who is worldly and polished in manner
un	**soph**	isticated	unsophisticated	lacking refinement or nuance

MEMORY

Mem comes from Latin and signifies memory.

Beginning	Root Word	Ending	New Word	Definition
	mem	ento	memento	keepsake or a reminder
	mem	orial	memorial	anything made or done to remember people or an event
	mem	oir	memoir	a biography often written by someone who knew the person well
re	**mem**	ber	remember	to recall in the mind

Rockin' Root Words Book 2 © Taylor & Francis Group • Permission is granted to photocopy or reproduce this page for single classroom use only.

MATCHING

Instructions: Match the root words to their definitions. Definitions can be used more than once.

Root Words

1. sci
2. mem
3. soph
4. intel

Definitions

a. knowledge
b. wisdom
c. memory

FILL IN THE BLANK

Instructions: Use the words for Lesson 7.5 to complete the sentences below.

1. I saved the ticket stubs as a _____ of my favorite team's miraculous win.

2. After a series of tests, it was found that her _____, or ability to apply her knowledge, was extremely high.

3. "Henry can be so _____ sometimes," she complained, adding, "He actually thought it was OK to wear jeans to the prom!"

4. The actor's wife wrote a touching _____ of his battle with cancer.

5. Although I knew in my _____ that it was wrong, I couldn't help lying about why I missed my curfew.

LESSON 7.6: SPIRIT AND CONSIDERATION

SPIRIT

The form signifying spirit is *anim*. It derives from Greek and Latin words for wind, air (necessary to all living things), breath, and soul and can be found in words like animal.

Beginning	Root Word	Ending	New Word	Definition
	anim	al	animal	living being (n.); of a kingdom of living things (adj.) that are not plants
	anim	osity	animosity	enmity, strong dislike
	anim	ated	animated	lifelike; lively
in	**anim**	ate	inanimate	lifeless; without life

CONSIDERATION

Put comes from Latin for consideration and shows up in words meaning thought or thinking.

Beginning	Root Word	Ending	New Word	Definition
dis	**put**	e	dispute	to argue, disagree, challenge (v.); a disagreement or debate (n.)
de	**put**	y	deputy	one empowered to act for another; a law enforcement officer; a legislator in some countries
re	**put**	e	repute	to consider or suppose
re	**put**	ation	reputation	public or general esteem; what others think of one's character
com	**put**	e	compute	to count, think, or consider mathematically

SYNONYM SEARCH

Instructions: Sort through the words in the word bank to find synonyms for the vocabulary words listed below. Write the synonyms on the lines next to the words they correspond with. Be careful—some of the words in the word bank will not be used!

Word Bank: lively, think verbally, lifeless, character, challenge, law enforcement, dislike, think mathematically, living being, consider

1. animosity _____

2. dispute _____

3. repute _____

4. inanimate _____

5. compute _____

6. animated _____

WEB QUIZ

Instructions: Try your hand at creating words! Connect the correct root word listed in the inner circle to the word parts listed in the outer circles. You may have to use a root word more than once!

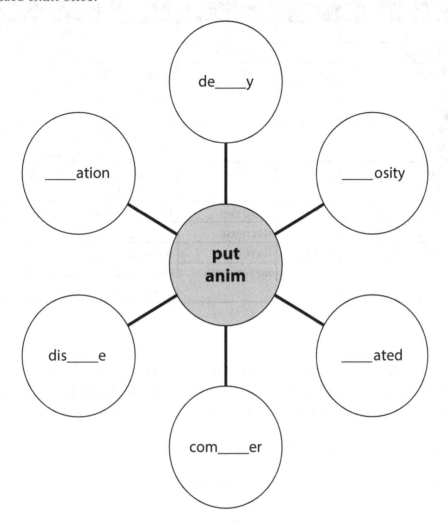

LESSON 7.7: GROWTH

Troph comes from Greek. *Cre* and *cru* are ancient word parts to describe growth.

Beginning	Root Word	Ending	New Word	Definition
a	**troph**	y	atrophy	a wasting away, especially of body tissues
dys	**troph**	y	dystrophy	faulty growth or development; atypical
	cre	ate	create	to grow or bring into existence
	cre	ature	creature	any living being; a strange or imaginary being
	cre	scent	crescent	a growing phase, as of the moon; sickle-shaped (adj.); a symbol of Islam (n.)
con	**cre**	te	concrete	something solid; formed into a solid mass; real, solid, specific, actual
in	**cre**	ase	increase	to make greater or grow
de	**cre**	ase	decrease	to lessen
in	**cre**	ment	increment	increase, addition
re	**cru**	it	recruit	grow again or new growth; enlist new friends (v.); a recently enlisted member

WORD SPLITS
. . . .

Instructions: The makers of a new dictionary want to break up some words into their word parts for their new edition, but need your help! Can you divide the following words into their word parts? Think carefully—a few words may be new to you!

1. creature: _____ + _____

2. creative: _____ + _____

3. decrease: _____ + _____ + _____

4. atrophy: _____ + _____ + _____

5. recruiter: _____ + _____ + _____

WHAT DOESN'T BELONG?
. . . .

Instructions: Choose the word in each line that *does not* mean the same as the first word.

1. **create**   to grow   to make   to destroy

2. **concrete**   fictional   real   solid

3. **dystrophy**   faulty growth   atypical development   typical growth

4. **increment**   subtraction   increase   addition

5. **recruit**   enlist   grow   release

LESSON 7.8: BREATHING

The roots *spir* (Latin) and *hal* can be found in words referring to breath or breathing and to words about the spirit of life.

Beginning	Root Word	Ending	New Word	Definition
re	**spir**	ation	respiration	breathing in and out
in	**spir**	ation	inspiration	breathing in; a prompting or encouraging
in	**spir**	e	inspire	to breathe in; stimulate, cause, guide, or motivate
	spir	it	spirit	life principle, soul, will, enthusiasm, mood, temperament; a divine force or being
per	**spir**	ation	perspiration	sweat
ex	**pir**	e	expire	to end, die, or cease
ex	**hal**	ation	exhalation	breathing out
in	**hal**	ation	inhalation	breathing in

PICK THE WORD

Instructions: Choose the best word or phrase that completes each sentence.

1. Our health teacher tried to teach us how to monitor our inhalation rate by

   breathing *(out, in, up)* very deeply, which helped us to relax.

2. My grandmother's stories of segregation *(expire, spirit, inspire)* me every day

   to work hard on my education.

3. After the grueling two-a-day workout for football, my gym clothes were

   soaked with *(respiration, perspiration, inspiration)*.

4. She *(exhaled, inhaled, perspired)* loudly, pushing the air out of her mouth with

   a big sigh of frustration.

WEB QUIZ

Instructions: Try your hand at creating words! Connect the correct root word listed in the inner circle to the word parts listed in the outer circles. You may have to use a root word more than once!

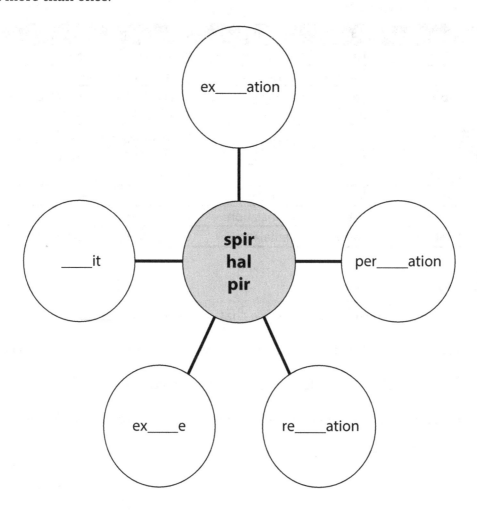

LESSON 7.9: SPEECH

THE CONVERSATION QUICKLY CHANGED FROM A DIALOGUE TO A MONOLOGUE

The roots *voc*, *loqu*, and *dic* derive from Latin for speech. *Ling* and *lang* come from Latin and French for voice. These roots appear in words for speech, calling, and words about words.

Beginning	Root Word	Ending	New Word	Definition
ad	**voc**	ate	advocate	to speak in favor of something (v.); a person who pleads or speaks for another
	voc	ation	vocation	occupation, business, or trade
	voc	alist	vocalist	singer
e	**loqu**	ent	eloquent	speaking with style
soli	**loqu**	y	soliloquy	in drama, a character's speech heard only by the audience that reveals a character's inner thoughts
	dict	ator	dictator	a ruler with absolute power to command
e	**dict**		edict	an official public proclamation or decree
bi	**ling**	ual	bilingual	speaking two languages
	ling	o	lingo	a dialect, jargon, or technical language unfamiliar to non-users
	lang	uage	language	system of verbal and/or written communication shared by a group

MATCHING

Instructions: Match the words to their definitions.

Words	Definitions
1. vocation	a. official proclamation
2. lingo	b. speaking with style
3. edict	c. occupation
4. eloquent	d. jargon

ALL MIXED UP

Instructions: Help! The following word parts were all mixed up in the dictionary. Connect the word parts by drawing lines between the boxes. Then, write the correct words in the lines next to their definitions. Be careful! Some of the connections can be tricky: You only want to find words that match the definitions below.

1. _____: communication system

2. _____: speak in favor of something

3. _____: speaking two languages

4. _____: singer

5. _____: ruler with absolute power

6. _____: reveals a character's inner thoughts

LESSON 7.10: PLEASE

Two groups of roots for please are *grac, grat, gree,* and *plea, pleas, and plac* (all from Latin). These root forms help determine when a word's meaning pertains to something pleasing, dignified, and being thankful.

Beginning	Root Word	Ending	New Word	Definition
	grac	e	grace	beauty of form, goodwill, favor; in Christianity, the love and favor of God shown to believers
dis	**grac**	e	disgrace	to bring shame or loss of reputation
	grat	itude	gratitude	thankfulness for favors or benefits
con	**grat**	ulation	congratulation	formal expression of good wishes for some achievement or good fortune
	grat	eful	grateful	thankful
a	**gree**		agree	to consent to or be in harmony with
	plea	d	plead	to argue a case in court or to beg
	pleas	ure	pleasure	happiness, satisfaction, delight, fun
	plac	ebo	placebo	literally, "I shall please" (Latin); a harmless preparation without medicine given to a patient
	plac	id	placid	calm, pleasing, or gentle

MAKE A WORD

Instructions: Match the correct root word and ending together to make five words. For example, the root word "non" and the ending "agon" together make the word "nonagon." The root words and endings can be used more than once.

Root Word	Ending	New Word
grac	ure	
grat	e	
plea	id	
plac	itude	
pleas	d	

FILL IN THE BLANK

Instructions: Use the words for Lesson 7.10 to complete the sentences below.

1. Over Thanksgiving break, our art teacher asked us to create a photo essay of the things we were _____ to have in our lives.

2. I read a really interesting article about how the singer's outburst on tour _____ her reputation.

3. In our biology class, we learned that many drug companies test medicines using two groups: one to get the medicine and one to get a _____, or a harmless mixture that the patient thinks is the medicine.

4. I couldn't help but _____ with my best friend—his argument made too much sense.

CHAPTER 7 REVIEW

CROSSWORD PUZZLE

CLUES:

ACROSS

1. living being
5. awareness, thinking, awake
6. speak on behalf of another
9. proclamation, decree
10. breathing in
15. display for the public to see
17. the face and its features
18. prickling sensation

DOWN

2. repetition of the same tone
3. disagreement
4. in harmony or agreement
7. to bring shame
8. love of wisdom
11. enlist
12. to beg
13. bring into existence
14. device to measure changes in the environment
16. sensitivity

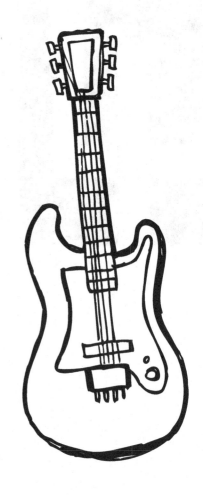

CHAPTER 8

Family, Home Life, and Religion

Our immediate family generally consists of mothers, fathers, brothers, and sisters. When people go to college, many young women join a sorority (sisterhood) and many young men join a fraternity (brotherhood). Marriage and children follow. Roman home life centered on the father, or the *pater familias*. He would decide whether you would go to school, who and when you would marry, and all other important decisions that involved the entire family. That doesn't mean the *mater familias* or mother was without influence. In fact, Roman history is filled with accounts of powerful women who constituted the real "power behind the throne."

Also, for many, an important part of family life is religion, the tenets (beliefs) of which are reinforced by attending religious services at the place of worship.

LESSON 8.1: SELF, MAN, AND WOMAN

SELF

The Greek roots for self are *auto* and *aut*.

Beginning	Root Word	Ending	New Word	Definition
	auto	mation	automation	a self-operating automatic system
	auto	nomy	autonomy	self-rule, independence
	aut	opsy	autopsy	medical procedure done to find out the cause of death

MAN

Anthrop derives from Greek to mean man and forms the roots of words that refer to humankind. *Homo* and *homi* also refer to humankind.

Beginning	Root Word	Ending	New Word	Definition
	anthrop	ology	anthropology	the study of human beings and past civilizations
mis	**anthrop**	e	misanthrope	one who hates mankind
	homi	cide	homicide	the crime of killing a human being
	homo	sapiens	Homo sapiens	scientific species name for humankind

WOMAN

Gyn comes from Greek to mean woman. The Latin base for female is *femin*.

Beginning	Root Word	Ending	New Word	Definition
	gyn	ecology	gynecology	the study of diseases particular to women
miso	**gyn**	y	misogyny	hatred for women
	femin	ine	feminine	being womanly; pertaining to women
	femin	ism	feminism	a movement that promotes equal political, social, and economic rights for women

Rockin' Root Words Book 2 © Taylor & Francis Group • Permission is granted to photocopy or reproduce this page for single classroom use only.

MATCHING

Instructions: Match the root words to their definitions. Definitions can be used more than once.

Root Words

1. femin
2. anthrop
3. auto
4. homi
5. gyn

Definitions

a. self
b. woman
c. man

ANALOGIES

Instructions: Using the words and definitions in this lesson, choose the best word to finish each analogy.

1. masculine : men : : feminine : _____

2. _____ : study of mankind : : psychology : study of the mind

3. _____ : self-rule : : democracy : rule by the people

4. misogynist : women : : misanthrope : _____

LESSON 8.2: FATHER, MOTHER, AND CHILD

FATHER

Patr/pater comes from Latin through French to describe fathers or fatherhood. This root also carries the additional meaning of the home.

Beginning	Root Word	Ending	New Word	Definition
	patr	iarch	patriarch	male head of the family or tribe
	patr	ilineal	patrilineal	showing descent or inheritance through the father or other male ancestor
com	**patr**	iot	compatriot	native or inhabitant of one's own country
	pater	nity	paternity	fatherhood

MOTHER

Matr/metro comes from Latin and refers to mothers and the state of motherhood.

Beginning	Root Word	Ending	New Word	Definition
	matr	iculate	matriculate	to enroll in school or college
	matr	ix	matrix	mold, womb, or underlying substance or form
	matr	iarch	matriarch	a mother as the head of the family, clan, or tribe
alma	**mater**		alma mater	literally, a "nourishing mother"; a term often applied by graduates to their colleges and universities
	metro	polis	metropolis	literally, "mother city"; a large city

CHILD

Ped comes from Greek to describe something that is related to children, deals with children, or is childish. This root also carries connotations of learning or study.

Beginning	Root Word	Ending	New Word	Definition
encyclo	**ped**	ia	encyclopedia	a book that covers all branches of knowledge
	ped	iatrician	pediatrician	physician specializing in children's diseases and health
	ped	igree	pedigree	genealogical chart of a family tree

WEB QUIZ

Instructions: Try your hand at creating words! Connect the correct root word listed in the inner circle to the word parts listed in the outer circles. You may have to use a root word more than once!

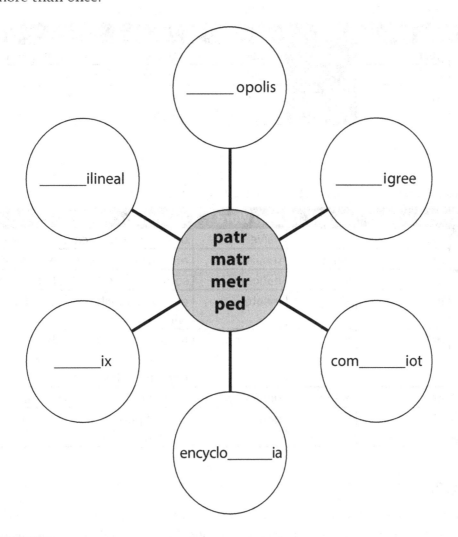

PICK THE WORD

Instructions: Choose the best word or phrase that completes each sentence.

1. My family's (*pediatrician, encyclopedia, pedigree*) is very rich in history; we can trace our ancestors back to the Native Americans.

2. After high school, I plan to (*matriarch, matriculate, matrix*) in my local community college.

3. After the death of my grandfather, my uncle became the (*patriarch, paternity, matriarch*) of our family, as per our Vietnamese traditions.

4. I would love to become a (*compatriot, alma mater, pediatrician*) someday and specialize in the diseases that affect children in poorer countries.

LESSON 8.3: PREGNANCY AND BIRTH

PREGNANCY

Gest comes from Latin and means carry, bear, or bring forth.

Beginning	Root Word	Ending	New Word	Definition
sug	**gest**		suggest	to mention as something to think over
in	**gest**		ingest	to take in; to eat
con	**gest**		congest	literally, "carry together"; to clog, to fill to excess

BIRTH

The roots for birth and the newly born are *nai*, *nat*, and *gen*.

Beginning	Root Word	Ending	New Word	Definition
	nai	ve	naïve	unsophisticated; childlike; lacking experience
re	**nai**	ssance	renaissance	rebirth, as of arts and learning in Europe
	nat	ional	national	something pertaining to a country as a whole
in	**nat**	e	innate	describes abilities or traits that one is born with
re	**gen**	erate	regenerate	to replace or recreate that which has been destroyed or damaged (like geckos, which regenerate lost limbs)
	gen	ealogy	genealogy	a chart or history of a person or family
	gen	try	gentry	class of people of high but not noble social standing

WORD SPLITS

Instructions: The makers of a new dictionary want to break up some words into their word parts for their new edition, but need your help! Can you divide the following words into their word parts? Think carefully—a few words may be new to you!

1. suggest: _____ + _____

2. digest: _____ + _____

3. regenerate: _____ + _____ + _____

4. innate: _____ + _____ + _____

5. native: _____ + _____

ALL MIXED UP

Instructions: Help! The following word parts were all mixed up in the dictionary. Connect the word parts by drawing lines between the boxes. Then, write the correct words in the lines next to their definitions. Be careful! Some of the connections can be tricky: You only want to find words that match the definitions below.

1. _____: to eat

2. _____: people of high, but not noble, standing

3. _____: lacking experience

4. _____: history of a family

5. _____: to clog

6. _____: rebirth

LESSON 8.4: Home

The roots for home are *dom* (Latin) and *eco* (Greek). *Cam* and *cham* are Greek for room.

Beginning	Root Word	Ending	New Word	Definition
con	**dom**	inium	condominium	jointly owned property or apartment building
	dom	inate	dominate	to rule over or to tower over
	dom	ain	domain	territory under one's control; field of activity or influence
	eco	nomy	economy	management of finances and other resources of a household, business, or nation
	eco	system	ecosystem	system made up of a community and its relationships
	cam	araderie	camaraderie	brotherhood, friendship
bi	**cam**	eral	bicameral	having two chambers, such as in state legislative assemblies
	cham	ber	chamber	vaulted room with an arched roof
	cham	berlain	chamberlain	someone who manages a royal household

CHANGE IT UP

Instructions: Replace the underlined word or words in each sentence with one of the vocabulary words in the word bank.

Word Bank: chamberlain, economy, condominium, camaraderie

1. The <u>finances and resources of the nation</u> has been very bad lately, with many companies going out of business.
2. We stayed in my grandmother's new <u>jointly owned property</u> when we visited her in Miami this summer.
3. I couldn't help but feel a sense of <u>brotherhood</u> with my future teammates after we went through 3 hours of tough tryouts.
4. It was easy to spot the culprit in the mystery story—the <u>person managing a royal household</u> had access to the king, queen, and the secret passageways, making it easy for him to commit the crime.

WEB QUIZ

Instructions: Try your hand at creating words! Connect the correct root word listed in the inner circle to the word parts listed in the outer circles. You may have to use a root word more than once!

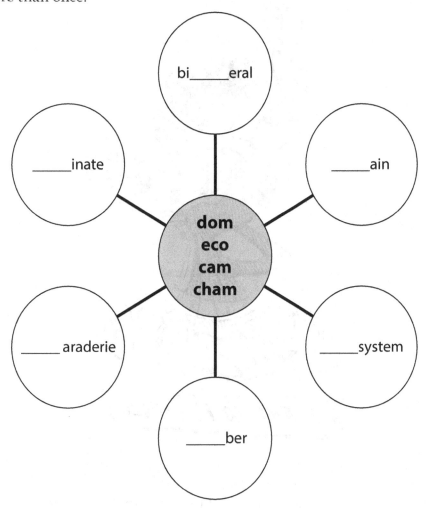

LESSON 8.5: FIRE

FLAMINGO FLAMENCO

The roots for fire are *volcan*, *flam* (Latin for burning), *ign* (Latin), and *pyr* (Greek).

Beginning	Root Word	Ending	New Word	Definition
	volcan	o	volcano	burning mountain, such as Mt. Etna in Sicily
	volcan	ic	volcanic	pertaining to volcanoes
	flam	mable	flammable	easily able to catch fire
	flam	boyant	flamboyant	architectural curves that are wavy and flamelike; a showy person
	flam	ingo	flamingo	tropical bird with pink to scarlet feathers
	flam	enco	flamenco	Spanish gypsy style of dance
	ign	ition	ignition	a firing or sparking of the explosive mixture of fuel and air in an engine
	ign	eous	igneous	fiery; of rocks produced by fire
	pyr	e	pyre	wooden pile for cremation of a body
	pyr	ite	pyrite	"firestone" or fool's gold; an iron mineral

WEB QUIZ

Instructions: Try your hand at creating words! Connect the correct root word listed in the inner circle to the word parts listed in the outer circles. You may have to use a root word more than once!

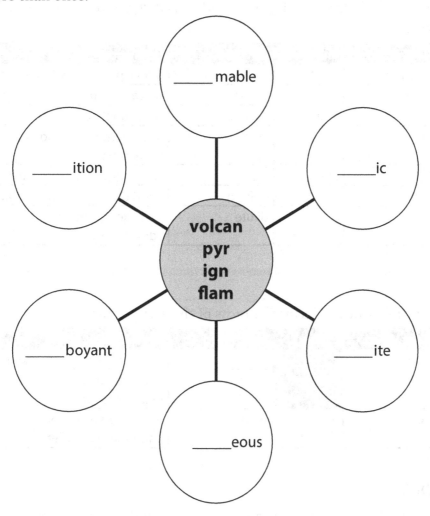

GUESS THE MEANING

Instructions: For each word below, guess its meaning, writing your guess in the second column. Then, look up the word in a dictionary and write the real meaning in the third column.

Word	I think it means . . .	It really means . . .
inflammable		
pyrotechnics		
flamed		
flameproof		
ignite		

LESSON 8.5: WASHING AND GARMENTS

WASHING

The roots for washing and cleaning are *laund*, *lav*, *lot*, *lug*, and *lut*, and all come from French and Latin.

Beginning	Root Word	Ending	New Word	Definition
	laund	romat	laundromat	public place for washing clothes
	laund	er	launder	to wash clothes or do laundry
	lav	atory	lavatory	washroom; room with a sink and toilet
	lav	ish	lavish	to be generous, prodigious, or extravagant in spending
	lot	ion	lotion	liquid medicine or cosmetic
de	**lug**	e	deluge	flood or downpour; wash away
di	**lut**	e	dilute	to make something less concentrated by adding water

GARMENT

Vest comes from Latin and forms the roots of these words for clothing.

Beginning	Root Word	Ending	New Word	Definition
	vest		vest	a robe or a short-sleeved garment
in	**vest**		invest	to clothe or cover; to use money to produce income; to furnish
tra	**vest**	y	travesty	a ridiculous dress or disguise; a poor imitation or mockery

MAKE A WORD

Instructions: Match the correct beginnings, root words, and endings together to make five words. For example, the root word "non" and the ending "agon" together make the word "nonagon." The beginnings, root words, and endings can be used more than once.

Beginning	Root Word	Ending	New Word
in	**lug**	e	
di	**lav**	er	
de	**lut**	ish	
	vest		
	laund		

THINKING ABOUT VOCABULARY

The lotus, an aquatic flower, is a sacred symbol for millions of people. Lotuses grow from mud and swampland pure and clean, causing them to be symbolic in many cultures. They smell sweet and are edible too! You can read about the lotus flower and how it's influenced cultures at http://www.platinumlotus.com/lotus_legend.html.

Instructions: Answer the following questions about the vocabulary for this lesson.

1. If someone spent quite a bit of money on unnecessary objects, you might say they lead what kind of lifestyle?

   _____

2. We use water to lessen the concentration of many household items, including bleach, tea, and lemonade. What is it called when you use water to change the consistency or strength of another liquid?

   _____

3. Pretend you've just been given $10,000. The only problem? To keep it, you must invest it. Choose three modern-day companies in which to invest your money. How much would you invest in each company? You may want to consult your newspaper or the New York Stock Exchange website (http://www.nyse.com) for help.

   _____

   _____

   _____

LESSON 8.7: RELIGION AND GOD

RELIGION

The root *religio* comes from the Latin and means the ritual worship of and respect for what is sacred.

Beginning	Root Word	Ending	New Word	Definition
	religio	n	religion	belief in a divine power to be obeyed and worshipped as the creator(s) and ruler(s) of the universe
	religio	us	religious	pertaining to religion, or its practice

GOD

Humankind has given several names to a power that some feel has made and is ruling the universe. The most common word roots for God in English are *the*, *theo*, and *div*, all from Greek.

Beginning	Root Word	Ending	New Word	Definition
	the	ism	theism	belief in a god or gods
pan	**the**	on	pantheon	collectively, all gods in a religion; a temple for all the gods
poly	**the**	ism	polytheism	the belief and practice of worshipping two or more gods
mono	**the**	ism	monotheism	the belief and practice of worshipping one god
	theo	logy	theology	a system of religious beliefs; the study of religious doctrines and beliefs
	div	ine	divine	pertaining to heaven; pertaining to theology (adj.); a member of the clergy or a theologian (n.); delightful
	div	inity	divinity	the quality of being godly or divine in nature
	div	a	diva	goddess; a female opera star

WEB QUIZ

Instructions: Try your hand at creating words! Connect the correct root word listed in the inner circle to the word parts listed in the outer circles. You may have to use a root word more than once!

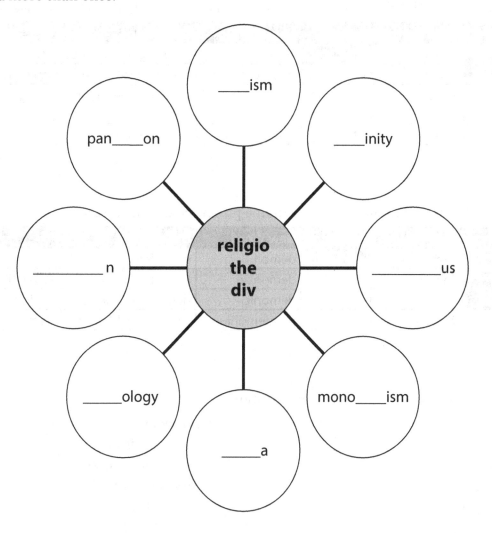

SYNONYM SEARCH

Instructions: Sort through the words in the word bank to find synonyms for the vocabulary words listed below. Write the synonyms on the lines next to the words they correspond with. Be careful—some of the words in the word bank will not be used!

Word Bank: temple, belief in many gods, goddess, being godly, study of religion, delightful, belief in one god, practice of religion, belief in a divine power

1. diva _____

2. religion _____

3. monotheism _____

4. divine _____

5. polytheism _____

LESSON 8.8: MESSENGER AND DEMON

MESSENGER

Angel (Greek and Latin) finds its way into words that refer to divine messengers.

Beginning	Root Word	Ending	New Word	Definition
	angel		angel	messenger of God; a supernatural being
	angel	ic	angelic	a messenger of God; completely innocent
ev	**angel**	ist	evangelist	messenger who "brings the good news" of the gospels
telev	**angel**	ist	televangelist	television preacher

DEMON

Demon (Greek and Latin) refers to a divine power, fate, god, and an evil spirit.

Beginning	Root Word	Ending	New Word	Definition
	demon		demon	evil spirit
	demon	ize	demonize	to portray someone as evil or threatening
	demon	ic	demonic	demon-like nature, pertaining to demons
pan	**demon**	ium	pandemonium	a state of wild uproar; chaos

MATCHING

Instructions: Match the words to their definitions.

Words	Definitions
1. angel	a. pertaining to demons
2. demon	b. television preacher
3. demonic	c. messenger of God
4. televangelist	d. evil spirit

FILL IN THE BLANK

Instructions: Use the words for Lesson 8.8 to complete the sentences below.

1. My puppy looked up at me with an _____ expression that

    completely denied the huge mess she had made tearing up the newspaper.

2. The streets were filled with a sense of _____ as people

    tried to escape the burning apartment building.

3. An _____ attempts to spread a message about the

    teachings of the Bible to the public.

4. Her rumors seemed to _____ my reputation; before I

    knew it, people began treating me as if I were a bully.

LESSON 8.9: TEMPLE, HOLY, AND POPE

TEMPLE

Templ comes from Greek and is in words referring to sacred objects, places, and acts.

Beginning	Root Word	Ending	New Word	Definition
	templ	e	temple	building for prayers and worship
	templ	ate	template	mold or pattern
con	**templ**	ate	contemplate	to think deeply about a problem

HOLY

The Latin forms for holy are *hier*, *sanct*, and *sacr/secr*. These roots describe holy rule and sacred places, objects, and events.

Beginning	Root Word	Ending	New Word	Definition
	hier	archy	hierarchy	rule by a high priest; more generally, a sense of ranking in an organization
	hier	oglyph	hieroglyph	Egyptian writing system that used symbols to stand for sounds, words, and syllables
	sanct	uary	sanctuary	a safe haven; a particularly holy place in a church or temple
	sacr	ed	sacred	holy or blessed
de	**secr**	ate	desecrate	to disregard the sacredness of something; to destroy or harm something considered holy

POPE

Pont comes from Latin and means bridge.

Beginning	Root Word	Ending	New Word	Definition
	pont	iff	pontiff	the Pope; a high priest
	pont	ificate	pontificate	to speak in a "preachy," self-important way

MAKE A WORD

Instructions: Match the correct root word and ending together to make five words. For example, the root word "non" and the ending "agon" together make the word "nonagon." The root words and endings can be used more than once.

Root Word	Ending	New Word
pont	ate	
sacr	oglyph	
templ	ed	
hier	iff	
	e	

SCRAMBLER

Instructions: Unscramble each word listed below. Use the clues to help you decipher the words.

pnattoemelc
(think deeply)

ateedscre
(destroy something holy)

yantuscra
(safe haven)

ioancptitfe
(to speak in a self-important way)

aichyerrh
(ranking)

CHAPTER 8 REVIEW

ROOT WORDS PUZZLER

Instructions: Combine the puzzle pieces to build new words. If you'd like, cut the pieces out and paste them on another sheet of paper.

SENTENCES

Instructions: Now that you've finished your puzzle, use each of the words you put together in a complete sentence.

CHAPTER 9

Government and Society

We have a wide variety of governmental systems throughout the world, which vary from monarchies in countries such as Great Britain and Japan or dictatorships such as that in Venezuela. Then, there are theocracies, such as in Iran and communist countries such as China and Cuba. Finally, there are democracies in many countries like the United States and India.

LESSON 9.1: KING/QUEEN

The root for royalty, *reg*, refers to a king or queen, royal powers, or guiding or ruling.

Beginning	Root Word	Ending	New Word	Definition
	reg	alia	regalia	royal status, power, or privileges shown by ceremonial dress, insignia, or emblems
	reg	ale	regale	to provide a feast or delight with something pleasing or amusing
	reg	al	regal	royal, like a monarch
	reg	ina	regina	queen (from Latin)
	reg	ime	regime	form of government or rule; period of time a person or system is in power
	reg	ent	regent	one who rules or governs for a king or other ruler; member of a governing board of a university or college
	reg	ion	region	territory, kingdom, or area
	reg	icide	regicide	killing of a king

WHAT DOESN'T BELONG?

Instructions: Choose the word in each line that *does not* mean the same as the first word.

1. **regalia**   ceremonial dress   ceremonial insignia   casual dress

2. **regime**   public   government   rule

3. **regale**   delight   lecture   amuse

4. **region**   territory   kingdom   governing board

5. **regent**   governing board   king   governor for a king

WEB QUIZ

Instructions: Try your hand at creating words! Connect the correct root word listed in the inner circle to the word parts listed in the outer circles. You may have to use a root word more than once!

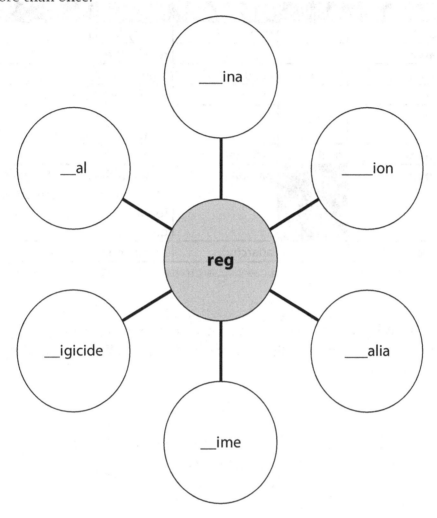

LESSON 9.2: GOVERNMENT BY RULE

The root is *arch* from the Greek for ruler or chief.

Beginning	Root Word	Ending	New Word	Definition
mon	**arch**	y	monarchy	rule by one king or queen
olig	**arch**	y	oligarchy	rule by the few
	arch	bishop	archbishop	high bishop
	arch	itect	architect	chief builder or designer
	arch	ipelago	archipelago	an area of a sea with many islands, like the Aegean Sea (also known as the "chief" sea)
	arch	rival	archrival	chief enemy
patri	**arch**		patriarch	father as the head of the family; an early Christian or Greek Orthodox bishop; a founder of a religion, business, or other group
an	**arch**	y	anarchy	rule by none, lawlessness, confusion

WEB QUIZ

Instructions: Try your hand at creating words! Connect the correct root word listed in the inner circle to the word parts listed in the outer circles. You may have to use a root word more than once!

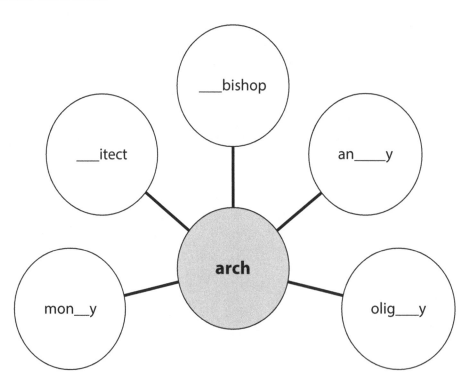

PICK THE WORD

Instructions: Choose the best word or phrase that completes each sentence.

1. If was as if total *(anarchy, oligarchy, monarchy)* had settled over the group; there was no order, no decisions, and a sense of lawless.

2. As the two teams were *(architects, archrivals, archipelagos)*, their football matches always drew enormous crowds.

3. Queen Elizabeth II of Britain is an example of a *(oligarch, patriarch, monarch)*.

4. The lead *(archrival, architect, archipelago)* gave us a tour of the impressive new skyscraper.

LESSON 9.3: POWER

Fort comes from Latin through French and means strong. *Crat* and *cracy* come from Greek for ruler.

Beginning	Root Word	Ending	New Word	Definition
com	**fort**		comfort	help, assist, soothe, give emotional strength
demo	**cracy**		democracy	rule of the people directly or through representatives; majority rule
bureau	**cracy**		bureaucracy	administration of government by departments; the officials of government as a whole
aristo	**cracy**		aristocracy	rule by the nobility or the best
klepto	**cracy**		kleptocracy	rule by thieves
pluto	**crat**		plutocrat	rich person who rules
techno	**crat**		technocrat	technical expert in the government

MATCHING

Instructions: Match the words to their definitions.

Words
1. comfort
2. technocrat
3. aristocracy
4. democracy

Definitions
a. rule by majority
b. rule by nobility
c. assist
d. technical expert

GOVERNMENT REUNION

Instructions: Your company is hosting the meeting of several important government officials. Unfortunately, the new intern mixed up the files and forgot to put each person's type or branch of government on his or her name tag. Using the clues given in the names on each tag, write what type or branch of government each person represents. (Hint! You may have to read the names out loud!)

LESSON 9.4: CITY/CITIZEN

Roots in this category are *urb* (Latin), *civ*, *cit* (Latin), and *polis* and *polit* (Greek and Latin). These roots describe cities, city life, relationships among people, and the management of groups of people.

Beginning	Root Word	Ending	New Word	Definition
	urb	an	urban	relating to cities and towns
	urb	ane	urbane	refined, elegant; cosmopolitan, as of city people
sub	**urb**	an	suburban	neighborhoods on the outskirts of cities
	civi	l	civil	respectful, courteous, polite
	civi	lization	civilization	country or people said to have a high stage of development; condition of being civilized or advanced
	cit	izen	citizen	person having full rights and duties in a country; civilian as opposed to a member of the military
	cit	y	city	large important center of activity with a population larger than a town or village
acro	**polis**		acropolis	"high city"; higher fortified part of an ancient Greek city
	polit	ician	politician	person holding or seeking public office
metro	**polit**	an	metropolitan	designating a city and its suburbs
cosmo	**polit**	an	cosmopolitan	representing many parts of the world; free from national or regional prejudices
	polit	e	polite	having good culture, taste, or manners

WORD SPLITS

Instructions: The makers of a new dictionary want to break up some words into their word parts for their new edition, but need your help! Can you divide the following words into their word parts? Think carefully—a few words may be new to you!

1. citizen: _____ + _____

2. impolite: _____ + _____ + _____

3. cosmopolitan: _____ + _____ + _____

4. suburban: _____ + _____ + _____

5. civilized: _____ + _____

CHANGE IT UP

Instructions: Replace the underlined word or words in each sentence with one of the vocabulary words in the word bank.

Word Bank: civilization, urbane, politician, city

1. My uncle is quite the <u>person seeking public office</u>; he beat his opponent for state senator by more than 10 percent.
2. Her impressive clothes and polished manners showed her <u>elegant or refined</u> taste.
3. I live in a <u>large center of activity</u> of more than 300,000 people.
4. Fascinated by the ancient Mayan <u>people with advanced development</u>, I asked my grandparents if we could visit Mexico and Central America this summer.

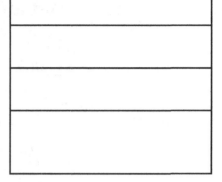

LESSON 9.5: LEAD

IT'S SIMPLE, WATSON. FROM THE CLUES PRODUCED I DEDUCE THAT THE VICTIM HAS BEEN INDUCED TO REDUCE.

The roots *duc* and *duct* come from Latin for "to lead." In addition, these roots refer to something that is made and something that leads the way.

Beginning	Root Word	Ending	New Word	Definition
pro	**duc**	e	produce	to make or bring into existence
re	**duc**	e	reduce	to lessen in size or number
in	**duc**	e	induce	to persuade; to lead into
de	**duc**	e	deduce	to trace or infer from logical reasoning
e	**duc**	ate	educate	to train; to help develop knowledge and skills
intro	**duc**	e	introduce	to originate or lead into
ab	**duct**		abduct	to take away a person by force or fraud; kidnap
de	**duct**		deduct	to take away or subtract
pro	**duct**	ive	productive	producing much; fertile, effective
con	**duct**		conduct	process of managing; the way one acts, behavior (n.); to show the way, guide, lead; to direct, manage, behave, transmit
via	**duct**		viaduct	a bridge or elevated road over a valley
aque	**duct**		aqueduct	large pipe for carrying water over a distance

MAKE A WORD

Instructions: Match the correct beginnings, root words, and ending together to make five words. For example, the root word "non" and the ending "agon" together make the word "nonagon." The root words and endings can be used more than once.

Beginning	Root Word	Ending	New Word
aque	duc	ate	
e	duct	e	
intro			
ab			
via			

WORD MATH

Instructions: Read the instructions in the box in order to create a new word by changing the word before it. Use the clues at the bottom of the box to help you create the new words.

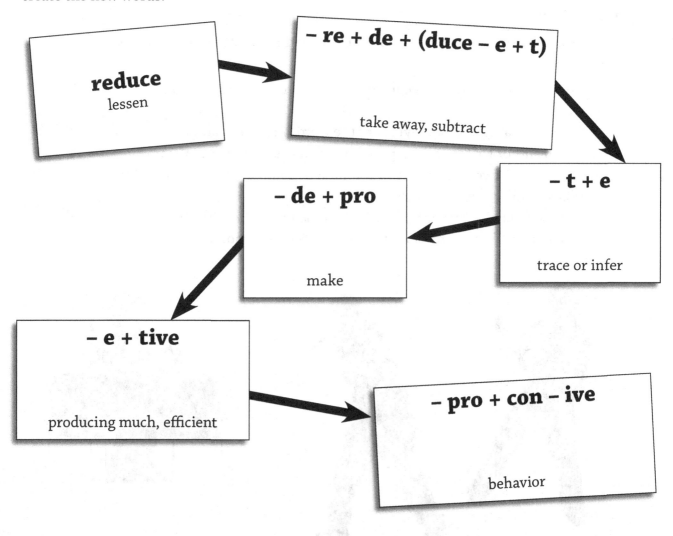

reduce
lessen

− re + de + (duce − e + t)

take away, subtract

− t + e

trace or infer

− de + pro

make

− e + tive

producing much, efficient

− pro + con − ive

behavior

LESSON 9.6: NAME

Roots for name are *nom* (Latin), *noun* (Latin), and *onym*.

Beginning	Root Word	Ending	New Word	Definition
astro	**nom**	er	astronomer	expert who studies the stars and planets or practices astronomy
de	**nom**	inator	denominator	the number below or to the right of the line of a fraction; a shared characteristic
	nom	inee	nominee	candidate chosen to run for an office or award
mis	**nom**	er	misnomer	wrong or misapplied name
pro	**noun**		pronoun	word that takes the place of a noun, such as I, we, them, they, it, and so on
pseud	**onym**		pseudonym	false name or pen name
ant	**onym**		antonym	word with opposite meanings (e.g., hot and cold)
syn	**onym**		synonym	words with the same or nearly the same meaning (e.g., fast and rapid)

TRUE OR FALSE

Instructions: Use the words for Lesson 9.6 to determine whether the following are true or false.

1. A misnomer is when someone uses the wrong name for an object or person.   T   F
2. A good example of synonyms are the words light and dark.   T   F
3. If an author writes under a pseudonym, she is using her real name.   T   F
4. To say that two things share a common denominator means that they have similar characteristics.   T   F
5. In the following sentence, "The boy jumped over the moon with excitement," the word "boy" is an example of a pronoun.   T   F

WEB QUIZ

Instructions: Try your hand at creating words! Connect the correct root word listed in the inner circle to the word parts listed in the outer circles. You may have to use a root word more than once!

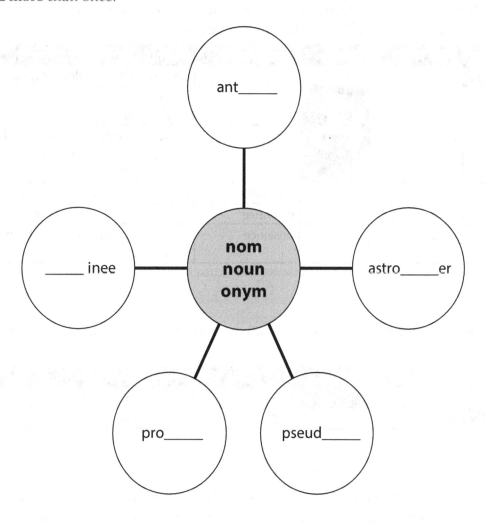

LESSON 9.7: TO WIN, WAR, AND PEACE

TO WIN

The Latin roots for winning are *vict* and *vinc* and refer to success, judgment, or proving. The root *vinc* takes on the additional meaning of an area.

Beginning	Root Word	Ending	New Word	Definition
	vict	ory	victory	win, success, complete and final supremacy
e	**vict**		evict	to recover property legally by forcing out a tenant, usually for nonpayment of rent
con	**vict**		convict	to judge and find guilty of an offense; a person found guilty of a crime and imprisoned
in	**vinc**	ible	invincible	unable to be defeated; unconquerable
con	**vinc**	e	convince	to overcome the doubts of; persuade
pro	**vinc**	e	province	area or territory; sphere or branch of learning

WAR

Bel comes from the Latin word *bellum* and means not only war, but also hostility and aggression.

Beginning	Root Word	Ending	New Word	Definition
re	**bel**		rebel	disobey, resist, defy
	bel	ligerent	belligerent	aggressive or combative

PEACE

Pac and *peas* come from Latin through French to mean peace. Magellan named the Pacific Ocean as such because it seemed so peaceful on his first voyage around the world in the 1500s.

Beginning	Root Word	Ending	New Word	Definition
	pac	ifist	pacifist	peacemaker; one who refuses participation in military service
	pac	t	pact	treaty or an agreement for making peace; an alliance between countries
	pac	ific	pacific	peaceful, quiet, tranquil, calm
ap	**peas**	e	appease	to bring peace or pacify, often by giving concessions to a potential enemy; to satisfy or relieve, as thirst by drinking water

MATCHING

Instructions: Match the root words to their definitions. Definitions can be used more than once.

Root Words

1. vict
2. peas
3. bel
4. vinc
5. pac

Definitions

a. war
b. win
c. peace

CHANGE IT UP

Instructions: Replace the underlined word or words in each sentence with one of the vocabulary words in the word bank.

Word Bank: invincible, pacifist, belligerent, appease, victory

1. The game ended in a hard-fought <u>win, success</u> for our team.
2. Our school counselor proved to be a great <u>peacemaker</u> when it came to solving our argument.
3. Garrett felt <u>unconquerable</u> as he won match after match in his tennis tournament.
4. I decided to <u>bring peace or pacify</u> her and let her choose the movie we saw on our first date.
5. My brother has such a <u>aggressive or combative</u> way of dealing with people; it really gets on my nerves!

CHAPTER 9 REVIEW

A GOVERNMENTAL WORD QUILT

Instructions: You've been commissioned to create a unique quilt to decorate the new International Government building in Washington, DC. The aim of the quilt is to educate visitors of the many different governmental vocabulary words. To create your quilt, choose four root words from this chapter, then list each word in the center block of the word quilt squares. For root word, choose four of your vocabulary words from this chapter that use that root, writing them in the second strip for each block. Then, write a definition for each word in the third layer of strips. Cut out your blocks and paste them into an arrangement on patterned or colored paper (to make your quilt backing).

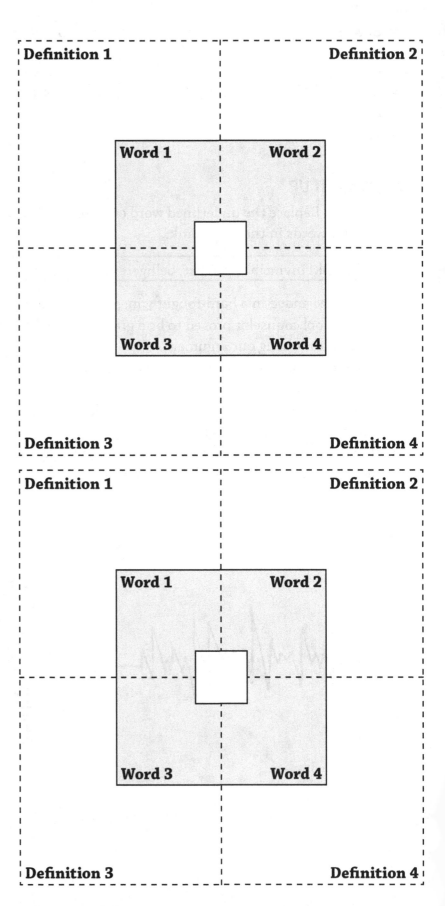

Name:_____ Date:_____

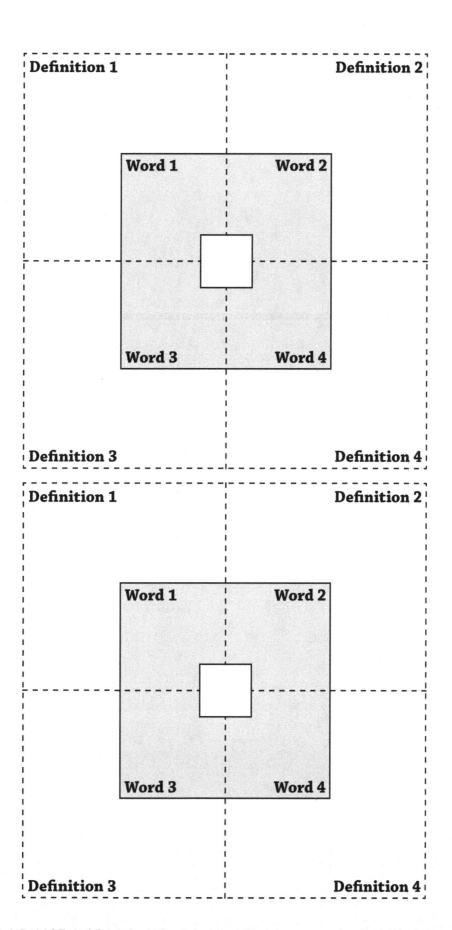

CHAPTER 10

Roots of Motion

This chapter covers the dozens of ways our bodies move, how we interact with our environment, and the words we borrowed from Greek and Latin to describe the ways we move.

LESSON 10.1: SIT AND LIE/RECLINE

SIT

Two roots help you determine when a word's meaning refers to sitting and position: *pon* and *pos*.

Beginning	Root Word	Ending	New Word	Definition
op	**pon**	ent	opponent	one that opposes; an adversary
pro	**pon**	ent	proponent	one who argues in favor of something
post	**pon**	e	postpone	to put something off until later
com	**pos**	e	compose	to put together or arrange
pur	**pos**	e	purpose	something set up as an object to be attained; a reason or motivation
ex	**pos**	e	expose	to lay open, uncover, or display
im	**pos**	e	impose	to force; to apply as required, like a tax; taking undue advantage

LIE/RECLINE

The roots for lying down or reclining are *cumb/cub*.

Beginning	Root Word	Ending	New Word	Definition
in	**cub**	ate	incubate	to maintain under certain conditions (usually warm), as for hatching eggs
	cub	e	cube	a solid object with six square-shaped and equal sides
	cub	icle	cubicle	small partitioned place within an office
in	**cumb**	ent	incumbent	current holder of an office or position
suc	**cumb**		succumb	to give in to a stronger force

FILL IN THE BLANK

Instructions: Use the words for Lesson 10.1 to complete the sentences below.

1. Although I knew I shouldn't, I decided to _____ my work on

   the project until the next weekend.

2. It was a tight race, but the _____ for governor managed to

   win over the dynamic, but inexperienced politician.

3. The British government tried to _____ a tax on items like tea

   and paper, leading to the Boston Tea Party.

4. We did a really cool experiment in biology that attempted to

   _____ and then hatch eggs using a warming oven.

WEB QUIZ

Instructions: Try your hand at creating words! Connect the correct root word listed in the inner circle to the word parts listed in the outer circles. You may have to use a root word more than once!

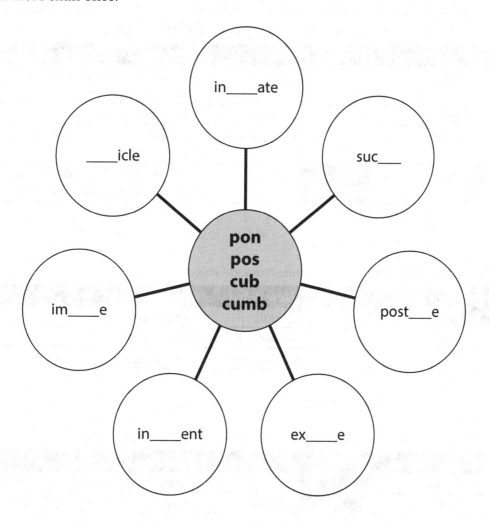

LESSON 10.2: CLIMB, WAVE, AND STRETCH

CLIMB

The roots for climb come from Latin in the form of *scen* and *scan*. The roots give form to words that indicate movement or vision over an area of some type.

Beginning	Root Word	Ending	New Word	Definition
de	**scen**	t	descent	the act of coming down from a high place to a low place
a	**scen**	t	ascent	upward movement
conde	**scen**	d	condescend	stooping to the level of one's supposed inferiors
	scan		scan	to check for recorded data, either on paper or with digital media like computers

WAVE

Und derives from Latin.

Beginning	Root Word	Ending	New Word	Definition
	und	ula	undula	tiny wave
ab	**und**	ant	abundant	plentiful, bountiful
red	**und**	ant	redundant	excessive or not needed

STRETCH

Tend and *tent* are the roots for stretching and they come from Latin and Greek.

Beginning	Root Word	Ending	New Word	Definition
dis	**tend**		distend	to stretch or enlarge from internal pressure
ex	**tend**		extend	to stretch out, lengthen, or enlarge
at	**tent**	ion	attention	giving considerable thought or care to
	tent	ative	tentative	something not fully worked out or developed
con	**tent**		content	satisfied; happy with what one has

MATCHING

Instructions: Match the root words to their definitions. Definitions can be used more than once.

Root Words

1. scan
2. tent
3. und
4. scen
5. tend

Definitions

a. stretch
b. wave
c. climb

Rockin' Root Words Book 2 © Taylor & Francis Group • Permission is granted to photocopy or reproduce this page for single classroom use only.

ALL MIXED UP

Instructions: Help! The following word parts were all mixed up in the dictionary. Connect the word parts by drawing lines between the boxes. Then, write the correct words in the lines next to their definitions. Be careful! Some of the connections can be tricky: You only want to find words that match the definitions below.

1. _____: upward movement

2. _____: to enlarge from internal pressure

3. _____: tiny wave

4. _____: giving considerable thought to

5. _____: stoop to an inferior's level

6. _____: plentiful

d

scen

tent

ant

ion

und

a

ula

scen

t

at

ab

conde

tend

und

dis

LESSON 10.3: BEND/FOLD

Flex and *flect* (Latin) note when a word's meaning signifies bending. *Plic* (Latin) carries the additional meaning of folding or bending.

Beginning	Root Word	Ending	New Word	Definition
	flex	ible	flexible	bendable
re	**flex**		reflex	automatic reaction, not controlled by will
in	**flex**	ible	inflexible	not bendable, brittle; not prone to change or compromise an opinion
de	**flect**		deflect	to turn aside from a fixed course
re	**flect**		reflect	to bend light back to its source, like a mirror; to show; to think about the past
accom	**plic**	e	accomplice	one who aids in a crime
du	**plic**	ate	duplicate	a second and exact copy
com	**plic**	ate	complicate	to confuse or make more complex or difficult
re	**plic**	ate	replicate	to duplicate, copy, reproduce, or repeat
multi	**plic**	ity	multiplicity	state of being varied; a vast number

TRUE OR FALSE

Instructions: Use the words for Lesson 10.3 to determine whether the following are true or false.

1. If your lawyer asks if you had an accomplice, he or she would like to know if you have an excuse that proves that you did not commit the crime. **T   F**

2. An inflexible opinion is extremely hard to bend or change. **T   F**

3. If something is complicated, it is easy to understand. **T   F**

4. Someone who thinks about or remembers prior events in his or her life is said to "deflect on the past." **T   F**

5. I would like to replicate the results of the experiment; therefore I should repeat it exactly. **T   F**

WEB QUIZ

Instructions: Try your hand at creating words! Connect the correct root word listed in the inner circle to the word parts listed in the outer circles. You may have to use a root word more than once!

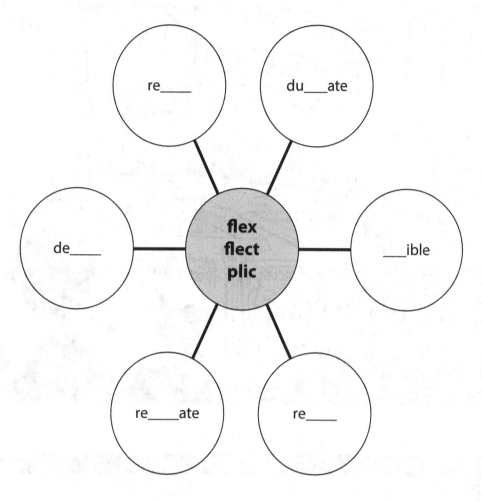

LESSON 10.4: CIRCLE

Circ and *cycl* come from Latin to mean circle.

Beginning	Root Word	Ending	New Word	Definition
	circ	a	circa	around or about in time
	circ	uit	circuit	a continuous path for electricity, like a circle
	circ	ulation	circulation	movement in a circle or circuit, especially the movement of blood through bodily vessels as a result of the heart's pumping action
	circ	us	circus	a show that often travels around and is performed in a large round tent
	cycl	ing	cycling	riding a bicycle or cyclical movement
	cycl	ist	cyclist	one who rides a bicycle or motorcycle
	cycl	ical	cyclical	moving or occurring in cycles
	cycl	one	cyclone	a violent tropical storm characterized by rapid inward circulation of air masses around a point of low pressure
uni	**cycl**	e	unicycle	cycle with one wheel
motor	**cycl**	e	motorcycle	cycle with a motor engine

MAKE A WORD

Instructions: Match the correct root word and ending together to make five words. For example, the root word "non" and the ending "agon" together make the word "nonagon." The root words and endings can be used more than once.

Root Word	Ending	New Word
circ	ist	
cycl	a	
	one	
	uit	
	ing	

THINKING ABOUT VOCABULARY

Circles and cycles make up much of our everyday vocabulary. We eat off circular plates, we use circle-shaped coins, and our births, deaths, and adolescence make up the human life cycle.
Instructions: Use the vocabulary words for this lesson to answer the following questions.

1. If a bicycle has two wheels and a unicycle only has one wheel, how many wheels are on a tricycle?

   _____

2. What is the scientific term for the movement of blood through your veins and arteries?

   _____

3. Circumference measures the distance around a circle or circular object. The formula for circumference is pi times the diameter of the circle ($\pi \times d$). Using the Internet, or with help from a coach, parent, or teacher, find the circumference of the following sports items: baseball, basketball, tennis ball, and golf ball.

Ball	Circumference
baseball	
basketball	
tennis ball	
golf ball	

LESSON 10.5: MOVE AND GO

MOVE

The root for move is the Latin *mov*.

Beginning	Root Word	Ending	New Word	Definition
	mov	ement	movement	act of moving; a series of activities aiming to promote a cause; a major musical division in a work
	mov	ie	movie	motion picture, film
re	**mov**	e	remove	to take away

GO

The roots *ced*, *cess*, and *ceed*, signifying to go, come from Latin.

Beginning	Root Word	Ending	New Word	Definition
pre	**ced**	e	precede	to go before or prior to
re	**ced**	e	recede	to go back or withdraw
re	**cess**	ion	recession	slowing of the economy; a withdrawal
se	**cess**	ion	secession	withdrawal, retirement, or separation from a country
ac	**cess**		access	approaching, getting, using; the right to go in or use; increase or growth; to gain, get, or retrieve data from
ne	**cess**	ary	necessary	describing something that one cannot do without; required; essential
ex	**cess**		excess	too much; more than needed; extra

MATCHING

Instructions: Match the words to their definitions.

Words

1. movement
2. access
3. remove
4. excess

Definitions

a. too much, extra
b. act of moving
c. the right to use
d. to take away

WORD MATH

Instructions: Read the instructions in the box in order to create a new word by changing the word before it. Use the clues at the bottom of the box to help you create the new words.

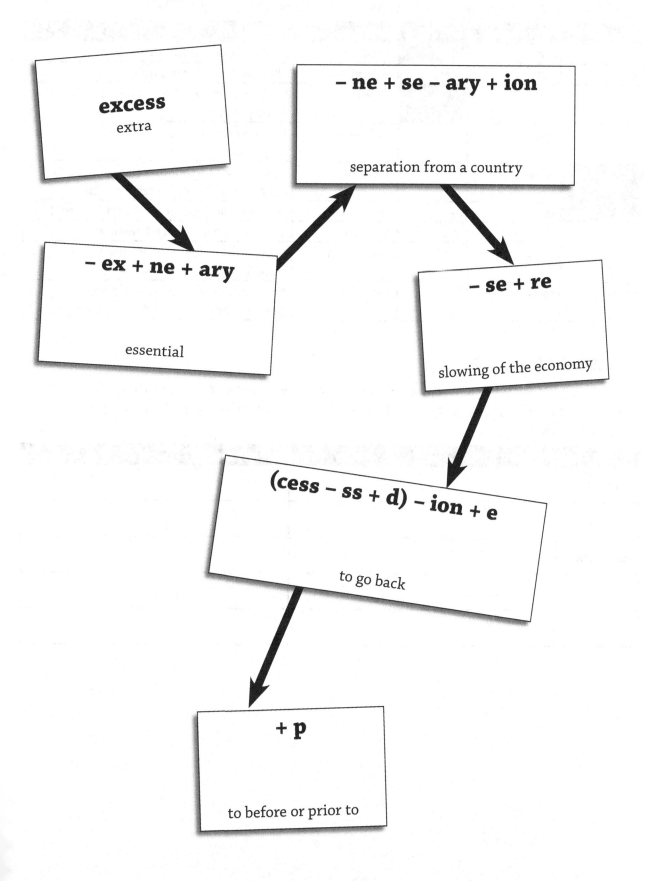

excess
extra

– ex + ne + ary

essential

– ne + se – ary + ion

separation from a country

– se + re

slowing of the economy

(cess – ss + d) – ion + e

to go back

+ p

to before or prior to

LESSON 10.6: SEND

The Latin roots for send are *mit* and *miss*. These roots give you a clue about when a word's meaning refers to entry, something sent out, and something allowed.

Beginning	Root Word	Ending	New Word	Definition
ad	mit		admit	to allow entry, as to a university
inter	mit	tent	intermittent	alternating, not continuous
per	mit		permit	to allow or make legal (v.); a license granting some privilege (n.)
e	miss	ary	emissary	agent who is sent to represent a country or corporation
	miss	ionary	missionary	a person sent to another part of the world to convert people to a religious faith
	miss	ile	missile	self-propelled rocket sent out to a target
o	miss	ion	omission	a failure to do; neglect; leaving out
per	miss	ion	permission	allowing or consenting; license to do something
trans	miss	ion	transmission	The act or process of transmitting or sending something, such as a message

GUESS THE MEANING

Instructions: For each word below, guess its meaning, writing your guess in the second column. Then, look up the word in a dictionary and write the real meaning in the third column.

Word	I think it means . . .	It really means . . .
omitted		
mission		
admittance		
committee		
dismiss		

WEB QUIZ

Instructions: Try your hand at creating words! Connect the correct root word listed in the inner circle to the word parts listed in the outer circles. You may have to use a root word more than once!

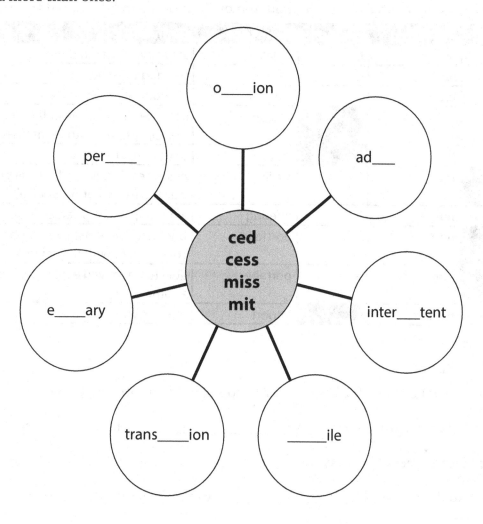

LESSON 10.7: BRING/CARRY

The roots for bring in or carry out are *lat*, *fer*, and *port*. The roots decipher when a word signifies something related, collected, told, removed, carried, and distanced from.

Beginning	Root Word	Ending	New Word	Definition
col	lat	e	collate	assemble pages in order
corre	lat	e	correlate	to bring together
legis	lat	e	legislate	to propose and pass laws
aqui	fer		aquifer	an underground bed or layer of earth, gravel, or porous stone that yields water
de	fer		defer	to put off, postpone
	fer	tile	fertile	describes something that will bear lots of fruit; be fruitful or productive
of	fer	ing	offering	a gift or present given as a matter of respect
	port	folio	portfolio	briefcase for carrying loose papers or a collection of writings or works of art
	port	able	portable	able to be moved easily from one place to another
im	port		import	to bring in

FILL IN THE BLANK

Instructions: Use the words for Lesson 10.7 to complete the sentences below.

1. The farmland proved to be quite _____; the second season produced a record harvest.

2. I created a beautiful _____ to showcase all of my artwork.

3. As a member of the student congress, I hope to help _____ new rules for the cafeteria and institute a spring dance.

4. She chose to _____ her job offer, deciding to travel for the summer and not work until the fall semester.

WEB QUIZ

Instructions: Try your hand at creating words! Connect the correct root word listed in the inner circle to the word parts listed in the outer circles. You may have to use a root word more than once!

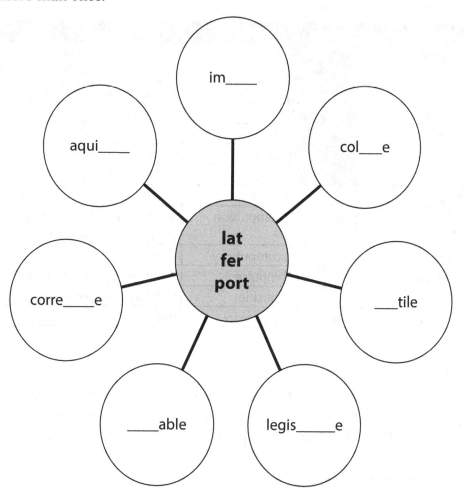

LESSON 10.8: PUSH

The roots for pushing are *peal*, *pel*, *puls*, *trud*, and *trus*. These roots identify when a word's meaning indicates a drive, to push against, or a thrust.

Beginning	Root Word	Ending	New Word	Definition
ap	peal		appeal	to call for help or sympathy, or a legal case to be heard again in court
re	peal		repeal	to withdraw or abolish a law
re	pel		repel	to push back or force away
dis	pel		dispel	drive away with force
ex	pel		expel	push out with force
pro	pel		propel	to push forward
	puls	e	pulse	heartbeat felt in neck or extremities
com	puls	ion	compulsion	an irresistible impulse to act, regardless of the rationality of the motivation
com	puls	ory	compulsory	required
im	puls	e	impulse	a sudden, difficult-to-resist desire to act
in	trud	e	intrude	to force in inappropriately
ex	trus	ion	extrusion	the act of pushing out by force

WORD SPLITS

Instructions: The makers of a new dictionary want to break up some words into their word parts for their new edition, but need your help! Can you divide the following words into their word parts? Think carefully—a few words may be new to you!

1. appeal: _____ + _____

2. repellent: _____ + _____ + _____

3. intrude: _____ + _____ + _____

4. intrusive: _____ + _____ + _____

5. compulsion: _____ + _____ + _____

WHAT DOESN'T BELONG?

Instructions: Choose the word in each line that *does not* mean the same as the first word.

1. **push out with force** expulsion expel repeal

2. **force or drive away** propeller dispel repel

3. **impulse** sudden urge desire to act push forward

4. **repeal** abolish approve withdraw

Rockin' Root Words Book 2 © Taylor & Francis Group • Permission is granted to photocopy or reproduce this page for single classroom use only.

LESSON 10.9: HURL/THROW

The root for throw is *ject*. It also helps decipher when a word's meaning deals with pushing into or against.

Beginning	Root Word	Ending	New Word	Definition
in	**ject**		inject	to push medicine into the body with a needle
ob	**ject**		object	to oppose
re	**ject**		reject	to throw away or to refuse to take
sub	**ject**		subject	a topic; in grammar, the part of the sentence that indicates who or what is doing the action; to bring under influence or power
ad	**ject**	ive	adjective	a class of words that modifies or describes nouns and pronouns
e	**ject**		eject	to throw out
pro	**ject**		project	thrown forward
pro	**ject**	or	projector	a machine that "throws" a picture onto the wall

MATCHING

Instructions: Match the words to their definitions.

Words
1. projector
2. adjective
3. subject
4. eject

Definitions
a. a topic
b. throw out
c. modifies or describes nouns and pronouns
d. machine that displays a picture on a wall

PICK THE WORD

Instructions: Choose the best word or phrase that completes each sentence.

1. The judge decided to *(reject, subject, project)* the defendant's evidence, based on the fact that it was not dated and could be fabricated.

2. While singing the final number in the school musical, I worked really hard to *(eject, subject, project)* my voice across the entire auditorium.

3. Kate wanted to *(subject, object, eject)* to Sari's opinion on the matter, because of their former feud, but Sari's reasoning was just too strong.

4. I have to *(object, reject, inject)* myself each night with insulin for my diabetes.

LESSON 10.10: BREAK/SHATTER

The roots for break/shatter are *frag*, *fract*, *rupt*, and *rout*. These roots identify when a word's meaning indicates incompleteness, something breakable, disorderliness, a part, or something changed away from the original path or plan.

Beginning	Root Word	Ending	New Word	Definition
	frag	ment	fragment	broken piece or a part broken off of a whole
	frag	ile	fragile	brittle or easily breakable; delicate
suf	**frag**	e	suffrage	the right to vote
	fract	ure	fracture	a broken bone
in	**fract**	ion	infraction	an instance of breaking a rule of law
ab	**rupt**		abrupt	sudden
bank	**rupt**		bankrupt	"broken bank;" a bank or company that has run out of money; a person who cannot afford to pay the bills
cor	**rupt**		corrupt	with broken morals; dishonest
dis	**rupt**		disrupt	to throw into confusion or disorder
	rupt	ure	rupture	to split or break open violently
	rout	ine	routine	a set of daily customary activities
	rout		rout	complete defeat, disorderly retreat

CHANGE IT UP

Instructions: Replace the underlined word or words in each sentence with one of the vocabulary words in the word bank.

Word Bank: suffrage, rout, infraction, bankrupt

1. Although projected to be close, the game against the Lobos turned out to be a <u>complete defeat</u>; we beat them 45–0.
2. Several insurance companies had to declare themselves <u>out of money</u> during the recession in 2009.
3. The <u>right to vote</u> movement thrust several women, such as Elizabeth Cady Stanton, into the public eye.
4. "Your behavior is a severe <u>breaking</u> of the rules," the principal stated. "Therefore, you have detention for 2 weeks."

WEB QUIZ

Instructions: Try your hand at creating words! Connect the correct root word listed in the inner circle to the word parts listed in the outer circles. You may have to use a root word more than once!

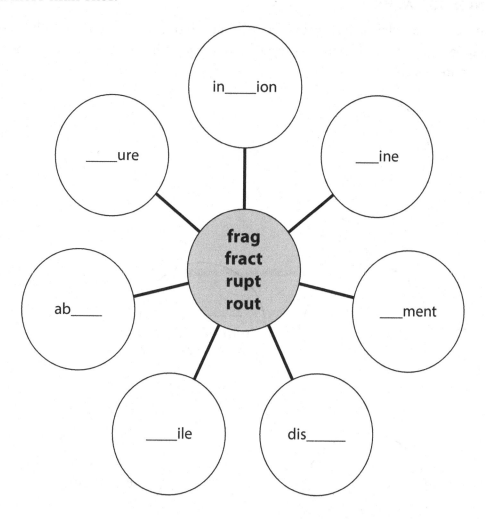

CHAPTER 10 REVIEW

BACK "WORDS" WEBS

Instructions: Using the definitions provided, fill in each outer circle on the webs below. Then, decide what each set of words has in common, writing the interconnecting theme for each web in the center circle.

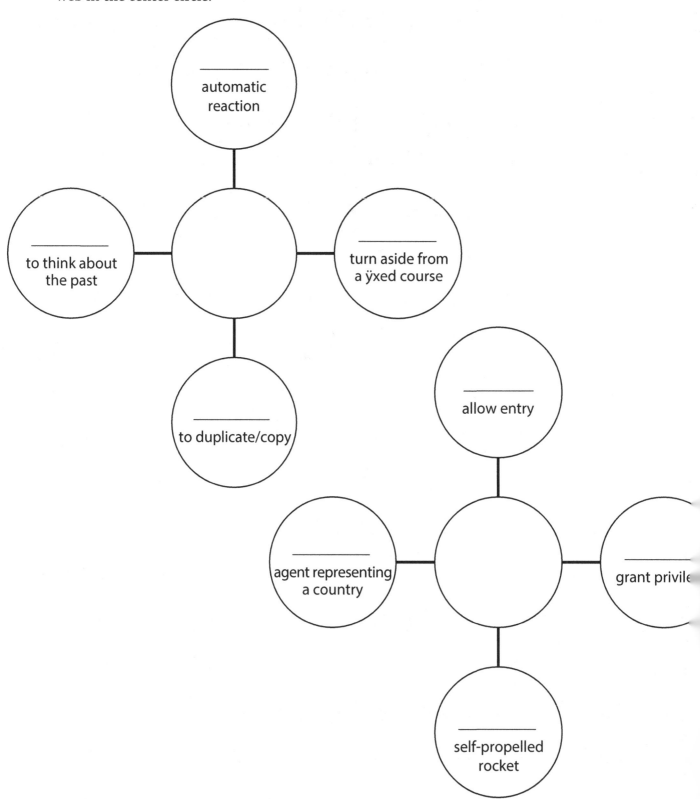

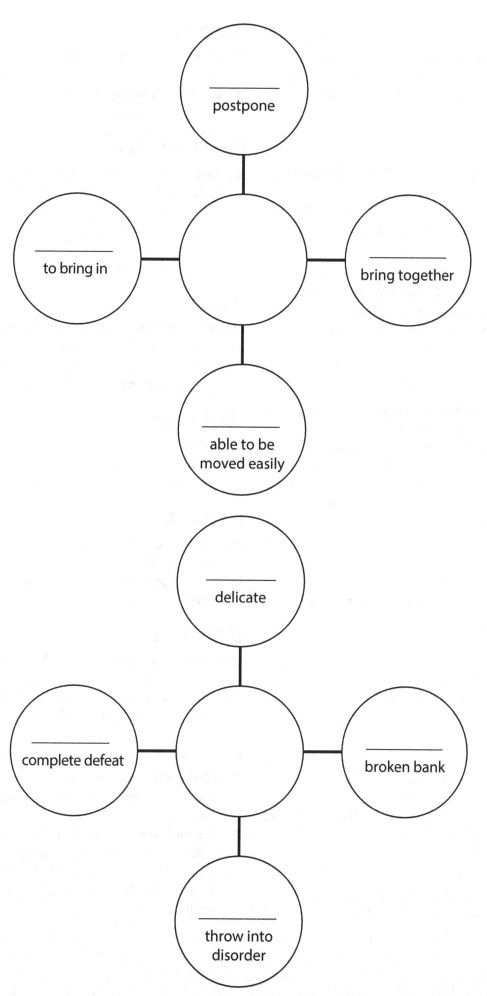

postpone

to bring in

bring together

able to be moved easily

delicate

complete defeat

broken bank

throw into disorder

LESSON 1.1

Web Quiz (Clockwise from top): numerable, numberless, numerology, renumber, numerate
Pick the Word: 1. renumber; 2. innumerable; 3. numerology

LESSON 1.2

Make a Word: semiannual, hemistitch, semifinal, demigod, hemiplegia, semilunar
Thinking About Vocabulary: 1. Answers will vary; 2. semiannual; 3. Answers will vary.

LESSON 1.3

Web Quiz (Clockwise from top): unanimous, unique, monogram, solitary, monologue
Fill in the Blank: 1. solitude; 2. unitard; 3. monogram; 4. unanimous

LESSON 1.4

Web Quiz (Clockwise from top): biceps, trident, duplicate, diphthong, trinity
Thinking About Vocabulary: 1. Answers will vary, but may include the story "The Three Little Pigs," or characters like the Three Blind Mice, the Three Musketeers, or the three billy goats Gruff; 2. trigonometry; 3. Answers will vary.

LESSON 1.5

Matching: 1. a; 2. b; 3. a; 4. a
Scrambler: quadrant, pentathlon, tetrarch, quatrain, quarterly, pentagon

LESSON 1.6

More or Less?: 1. more than; 2. less than; 3. less than
Web Quiz (Clockwise from top): heptad, septennial, octane, hexachord, octopus

LESSON 1.7

Make a Word: nonagenarian, decimeter, nonillion, decimate, decagon, nonet
Fill in the Blank: 1. nones; 2. decimate; 3. decathlete

LESSON 1.8

Matching: 1. b; 2. b; 3. a
All Mixed Up: 1. kilohertz; 2. centenarian; 3. kilobyte; 4. milliliter; 5. centurion

LESSON 1.9

Word Splits: 1. prima + donna; 2. proto + n; 3. pen + ulti + mate; 4. arch + aic; 5. arch + aeologist
What Doesn't Belong: 1. first; 2. secondary; 3. modern; 4. finished product; 5. final draft

CHAPTER 1 REVIEW

Number Sense: 1: monocle, unit; 2: duplicate, bivalve; 3: trinity, trident; 4: quadriplegic, tetrahedron; 5: pentagon; 6: sextant, hexachord; 7: septumvirate, heptad; 8: octane; 9: nonet; 10: decapod, decennial; 100: centigrade; 1,000: kilovolt, milligram

LESSON 2.1

Web Quiz (Clockwise from top): equality, isotope, equilibrium, equate, isosceles
Fill in the Blank: 1. equality; 2. equilibrium; 3. isotopes; 4. isometry; 5. equation

LESSON 2.2

Matching: 1. b; 2. a; 3. b
Synonym Search: 1. use both hands; 2. outlaw; 3. deny; 4. ignore; 5. uncommitted

LESSON 2.3

Make a Word: polymer, plus, polygon, multinational, plurilingual
Change It Up: 1. multiform; 2. plurilingual; 3. polygon; 4. polygraph

LESSON 2.4

Web Quiz (Clockwise from top): copious, panorama, holograph, cornucopia, pandemonium
Fill in the Blank: 1. cornucopia; 2. pantomime; 3. holographs; 4. Holocaust; 5. panoramic

LESSON 2.5

Web Quiz (Clockwise from top): microchip, minimize, mince, minimum, microbiology, minutiae
Adding Suffixes: Answers may vary, but should include definitions along the lines of the following: 1. to make legal; 2. short skirt; 3. to make official; 4. to make something individual; 5. small bus

LESSON 2.6

Make a Word: magnate, magnanimous, maximal, macroscopic, macronutrient

Pick the Word: 1. macrocosm; 2. maximize; 3. magnate; 4. magnitude

LESSON 2.7

Word Splits: 1. de + bas + e; 2. acro + stic; 3. e + long + ate; 4. a + bas + e; 5. pro + long

Thinking About Vocabulary: 1. acrophobia; 2. Answers will vary, but make sure students use the words correctly in their sentences; 3. Answers will vary, but the image should look like the Parthenon and include a caption with information about the ruins.

CHAPTER 2 REVIEW

Root Word Pyramid: Top Row: details; Second Row (L–R): summarize, maximal; Third Row (L–R): isosceles, generous, unimportant; Fourth Row (L–R): abundant, ambiguous, diminish, multinational

LESSON 3.1

Web Quiz (Clockwise from top): contemporary, chronology, tempo, synchronized, chronic

Thinking About Vocabulary: 1. Answers will vary, but may include fairy tales like Cinderella (with the clock striking midnight) and Sleeping Beauty (who must sleep for 100 years); 2. crony; 3. Answers will vary, but should include activities that require a tempo like running or dancing.

LESSON 3.2

Matching: 1. c; 2. a; 3. e; 4. f; 5. d; 6. b

What Doesn't Belong?: 1. final; 2. informed decision; 3. foremost

LESSON 3.3

Web Quiz (Clockwise from top): sequel, postsecondary, postbellum, consequent, postdate, consecutive

Fill in the Blank: 1. postdate; 2. sequel; 3. consecutive; 4. postsecondary; 5. consequent

LESSON 3.4

Word Splits: 1. equi + nox; 2. journ + ey; 3. meri + dia + n; 4. journ + alist; 5. noct + urne

All Mixed Up: 1. diary; 2. journal; 3. nocturnal; 4. adjourn; 5. dial

LESSON 3.5

Make a Word: monthly, lunate, lunatic, month, lunar

Fill in the Blank: 1. Monday; 2. lunacy; 3. semester; 4. lunate; 5. monthly

LESSON 3.6

More Often or Less Often?: 1. less often than; 2. more often than; 3. more often than

Web Quiz (Clockwise from top): annals, perennial, annual, annuity, biennial

CHAPTER 3 REVIEW

The Word Clock: 1. lunacy; 2. bicentennial; 3. tempest; 4. sequel; 5. annuity; 6. precede; 7. semester; 8. sojourn; 9. posthumous; 10. nocturnal; 11. prejudice; 12. meridian

LESSON 4.1

Web Quiz (Clockwise from top): superb, overthrow, epidemic, superstition, overboard, hyperbole, epidermis, hyperactive

Fill in the Blank: 1. superstition; 2. hyperactive; 3. overthrow; 4. epidemic

LESSON 4.2

Thinking About Vocabulary: Answers will vary, but may include: subdivision, substance, subscription, submarine, and submit; and underwear, underhand, underarm, underline, and underneath.

Web Quiz (Clockwise from top): subconscious, undercurrent, submerge, hypocrisy, underhanded, hypothermia

LESSON 4.3

Matching: 1. a; 2. a; 3. b; 4. a; 5. b; 6. b

Outside or Inside?: 1. introspect; 2. embassy; 3. eradicate; 4. engrave; 5. exhale; 6. eject; 7. index; 8. excavate; The words inside the circle should be: introspect, embassy, engrave, and index; the words outside the circle should be: eradicate, exhale, eject, and excavate.

LESSON 4.4

Word Splits: 1. peri + scope; 2. circum + scribe; 3. com + para + ble; 4. circu + it; 5. para + graph

Pick the Word: 1. moral; 2. periphery; 3. indirect; 4. circumvent

LESSON 4.5

Make a Word: The words are: advance, annex, allure, abduct, aggregate, apocalypse.

Analogies: 1. apothecary; 2. affluent; 3. hate; 4. adapt

LESSON 4.6

Matching: 1. b; 2. a; 3. a; 4. b; 5. a

Fill in the Blank: 1. perspire; 2. catastrophe; 3. dialogue; 4. decelerate

LESSON 4.7

Guess the Meaning: Answers will vary. Check your class dictionary or an online dictionary of your preference for the exact meanings.

Web Quiz (Clockwise from top): resurge, anachronism, anagram, reiterate, retort

LESSON 4.8

Matching: 1. d; 2. e; 3. f; 4. b; 5. c; 6. a

Scrambler: The unscrambled words are: synchronize, correlate, sympathy, combine, congruent, syllabus, coherent

LESSON 4.9

Guess the Meaning: Answers will vary. Check your class dictionary or an online dictionary of your preference for the exact meanings.

Web Quiz (Clockwise from top): anonymous, asymmetrical, nonprofit, illiterate, unspoken, insincere

LESSON 4.10

Fill in the Blank: 1. antagonist; 2. offensive; 3. counterclockwise; 4. obtuse; 5. oppression

Web Quiz (Clockwise from top): contrast, occult, antidote, offensive, object, counterbalance

CHAPTER 4 REVIEW

Word Bubbles: 1. co; 2. epi; 3. al; 4. hypo; 5. ana; 6. in; 7. de; 8. peri; 9. contra; 10. ex

LESSON 5.1

Web Quiz (Clockwise from top): figure, formless, configuration, surface, facet, formation

What Doesn't Belong: 1. real; 2. go out; 3. configure; 4. outdoors; 5. surface

LESSON 5.2

Make a Word: The words are: platform, orthotics, plane, orthodontist, plateau

Change It Up: 1. plateau; 2. plain; 3. orthopedic; 4. platypus

LESSON 5.3

Word Splits: 1. chrom + e; 2. chrom + osome; 3. poly + chrom + atic; 4. chrom + atology; 5. chrom + atist

Word Math: The words are: chromosome, monochromatic, chromatic, polychromatic, chromium

LESSON 5.4

Web Quiz (Clockwise from top): album, melancholy, Argentina, melanin, albumen, argentine

Fill in the Blank: 1. melanin; 2. albinism; 3. Argentina; 4. melancholy

LESSON 5.5

Matching: 1. a; 2. b; 3. b; 4. a; 5. a; 6. b

Thinking About Vocabulary: 1. misconception; 2. a bonus; 3. Answers will vary, but you should make sure the poem has at least five lines and is celebratory of the person's life. 4. Answers will vary. If a natural disaster has occurred recently in your area or is receiving widespread attention (such as the 2010 earthquake in Haiti), you may consider having your students actually campaign to collect items for the victims. If you wish, you can send your students' donations to the Red Cross for distribution.

LESSON 5.6

Word Splits: 1. homo + nym; 2. simil + e; 3. re + sembl + e; 4. as + simil + ate; 5. as + sembl + y

All Mixed Up: 1. ensemble; 2. simultaneous; 3. similar; 4. homogenize; 5. simulator; 6. assemble

LESSON 5.7

Synonym Search: 1. meaningful story; 2. foreigner; 3. different kinds; 4. pseudonym; 5. changeable; 6. hypersensitivity

Web Quiz (Clockwise from top): allergy, variant, alien, allegory, alias, heterogeneous, variation

CHAPTER 5 REVIEW

1. melancholy; 2. alienate; 3. diffuse; 4. configuration;
5. assimilate; 6. Albion; 7. deface; 8. chromatic;
9. orthotics; 10. debonair; Jumbled Word:
dysfunctional

LESSON 6.1

Pick the Word: 1. courage; 2. organ; 3. discord; 4.
encourage

Web Quiz (Clockwise from top): cardiac, discord,
courage, organism, record, disorganized, accord,
encourage

LESSON 6.2

Matching: 1. b; 2. a; 3. b

Analogies: 1. orthodontist; 2. captain; 3. drink/
beverage; 4. bullfighter

LESSON 6.3

What Doesn't Belong?: 1. ask; 2. release; 3. talking
a lot; 4. capture; 5. inability

Web Quiz (Clockwise from top): manner,
chiropractor, manufacture, caption, capture,
dexterity, manicurist

LESSON 6.4

Change It Up: 1. pedometer; 2. podiatrist; 3. octopus;
4. impediment

Word Math: pedestal, pedal, expedition, podium,
tripod

LESSON 6.5

Word Splits: 1. viv + acity; 2. zo + diac; 3. re + vit +
alize; 4. re + viv + al

Pick the Word: 1. zoology; 2. vital; 3. survivor; 4.
biosphere

LESSON 6.6

Fill in the Blank: 1. mortal; 2. terminate; 3. infinite;
4. eliminate

Web Quiz (Clockwise from top): infinite, immortal,
mortician, eliminate, finale, terminal, mortal

LESSON 6.7

Matching: 1. c; 2. a; 3. d; 4. b

Thinking About Vocabulary: 1. omnivore; 2.
corporation; 3. sarcastic; 4. Answers will vary.
Traditional elements usually include masks,
parades, dancing, and specific foods.

CHAPTER 6 REVIEW

Create a Comic: Answers will vary. Make sure
students use at least seven words from the
chapter in their comic strip.

LESSON 7.1

Pick the Word: 1. revise; 2. stethoscope; 3. spectacle;
4. obvious

Web Quiz (Clockwise from top): visage,
stethoscope, provide, spectacles, supervisor,
evident, microscope

LESSON 7.2

Analogies: 1. audible; 2. tone; 3. unpleasant or noisy;
4. percussion

Web Quiz (Clockwise from top): xylophone,
audition, tone, audible, monotone, sonogram,
sonic

LESSON 7.3

Word Splits: 1. in + tact; 2. tact + ful; 3. con + ting +
ent; 4. tact + ile; 5. in + tang + ible

Word Math: The words are: tangential, tangible,
tingle, contingent

LESSON 7.4

Guess the Meaning: Answers will vary. Check your
class dictionary or an online dictionary of your
preference for the exact meanings.

Web Quiz (Clockwise from top): dissent,
sentiment, sensitive, sentinel, sensible, nonsense

LESSON 7.5

Matching: 1. a; 2. c; 3. b; 4. a

Fill in the Blank: 1. memento; 2. intelligence; 3.
unsophisticated; 4. memoir; 5. conscience

LESSON 7.6

Synonym Search: 1. dislike; 2. challenge; 3. consider;
4. lifeless; 5. think mathematically; 6. lively

Web Quiz (Clockwise from top): deputy, animosity,
animated, computer, dispute, animation

LESSON 7.7

Word Splits: 1. cre + ature; 2. cre + ative; 3. de + cre +
ase; 4. a + troph + y; 5. re + cru + iter

What Doesn't Belong?: 1. to destroy; 2. fictional; 3.
typical growth; 4. subtraction; 5. release

LESSON 7.8

Pick the Word: 1. in; 2. inspire; 3. perspiration; 4. exhaled

Web Quiz (Clockwise from top): exhalation, perspiration, respiration, expire or exhale, spirit

LESSON 7.9

Matching: 1. c; 2. d; 3. a; 4. b

All Mixed Up: 1. language; 2. advocate; 3. bilingual; 4. vocalist; 5. dictator; 6. soliloquy

LESSON 7.10

Make a Word: The words are: grace, gratitude, plead, placid, pleasure

Fill in the Blank: 1. grateful; 2. disgraced; 3. placebo; 4. agree

CHAPTER 7 REVIEW

Crossword Puzzle: Across: 1. animal, 5. conscious, 6. advocate, 9. edict, 10. inhalation, 15. spectacle, 17. visage, 18. tingle; Down: 2. monotone; 3. dissent; 4. consonant; 7. disgrace; 8. philosophy; 11. recruit; 12. plead; 13. create; 14. sensor; 16. tact

LESSON 8.1

Matching: 1. b; 2. c; 3. a; 4. c; 5. b

Analogies: 1. women; 2. anthropology; 3. autonomy; 4. mankind

LESSON 8.2

Web Quiz (Clockwise from top): metropolis, pedigree, compatriot, encyclopedia, matrix, patrilineal

Pick the Word: 1. pedigree; 2. matriculate; 3. patriarch; 4. pediatrician

LESSON 8.3

Word Splits: 1. sug + gest; 2. di + gest; 3. re + gen + erate; 4. in + nat + e; 5. nat + ive

All Mixed Up: 1. ingest; 2. gentry; 3. naïve; 4. genealogy; 5. congest; 6. renaissance

LESSON 8.4

Change It Up: 1. economy; 2. condominium; 3. camaraderie; 4. chamberlain

Web Quiz (Clockwise from top): bicameral, domain, ecosystem, chamber, camaraderie, dominate

LESSON 8.5

Web Quiz (Clockwise from top): flammable, volcanic, pyrite or ignite, igneous, flamboyant, ignition

Guess the Meaning: Answers will vary. Check your class dictionary or an online dictionary of your preference for the exact meanings.

LESSON 8.6

Make a Word: The words are: invest, dilute, deluge, lavish, launder

Thinking About Vocabulary: 1. lavish; 2. dilute; 3. Answers will vary. Make sure the companies are actual companies and the students' investments add up to $10,000.

LESSON 8.7

Web Quiz (Clockwise from top): theism, divinity, religious, monotheism, diva, theology, religion, pantheon

Synonym Search: 1. goddess; 2. belief in a divine power; 3. belief in one god; 4. delightful; 5. belief in many gods

LESSON 8.8

Matching: 1. c; 2. d; 3. a; 4. b

Fill in the Blank: 1. angelic; 2. pandemonium; 3. evangelist; 4. demonize

LESSON 8.9

Make a Word: The words are: pontiff, sacred, template, temple, hieroglyph

Scrambler: contemplate, desecrate, sanctuary, pontificate, hierarchy

CHAPTER 8 REVIEW

Root Words Puzzler: The words are: autopsy, sanctuary, demonize, divinity, invest, launder, volcanic, domain, national, paternity

Sentences: Answers will vary.

LESSON 9.1

What Doesn't Belong?: 1. casual dress; 2. public; 3. lecture; 4. governing board; 5. king

Web Quiz (Clockwise from top): regina, region, regalia, regime, regicide, regal

LESSON 9.2

Web Quiz (Clockwise from top): archbishop, anarchy, oligarchy, monarchy, architect

Pick the Word: 1. anarchy; 2. archrivals; 3. monarch; 4. architect

LESSON 9.3

Matching: 1. c; 2. d; 3. b; 4. a

Government Reunion: I. Steele: Kleptocracy; Dee Partment: Bureaucracy; P. Pulls-Choice: Democracy; Munn E. Baggs: Plutocrat; Ima Noble: Aristocracy; Teck Nichols: Technocrat

LESSON 9.4

Word Splits: 1. cit + izen; 2. im + polit + e; 3. cosmo + polit + an; 4. sub + urb + an; 5. civ + ilized

Change It Up: 1. politician; 2. urbane; 3. city; 4. civilization

LESSON 9.5

Make a Word: The words are: aqueduct, educate, introduce, abduct, viaduct

Word Math: The words are: deduct, deduce, produce, productive, conduct

LESSON 9.6

True or False: 1. T; 2. F; 3. F; 4. T; 5. F

Web Quiz (Clockwise from top): antonym, astronomer, pseudonym, pronoun, nominee

LESSON 9.7

Matching: 1. b; 2. c; 3. a; 4. b; 5. c

Change It Up: 1. victory; 2. pacifist; 3. invincible; 4. appease; 5. belligerent

CHAPTER 9 REVIEW

A Governmental Word Quilt: Answers will vary. Make sure that the words defined match the root word in the center of the squares.

LESSON 10.1

Fill in the Blank: 1. postpone; 2. incumbent; 3. impose; 4. incubate

Web Quiz (Clockwise from top): incubate, succumb, postpone, expose, incumbent, impose, cubicle

LESSON 10.2

Matching: 1. c; 2. a; 3. b; 4. c; 5. a

All Mixed Up: 1. ascent; 2. distend; 3. undula; 4. attention; 5. condescend; 6. abundant

LESSON 10.3

True or False: 1. F; 2. T; 3. F; 4. F; 5. T

Web Quiz (Clockwise from top): duplicate, flexible, reflect, replicate, deflect, reflex (Note that reflex and reflect may be switched in order.)

LESSON 10.4

Make a Word: The words are: circa, cyclist, cyclone, circuit, cycling

Thinking About Vocabulary: 1. three; 2. circulation; 3. baseball = 9 inches; basketball = 29 to 30 inches; tennis ball = 2.5 to 2.625 inches; golf ball = 1.68 inches

LESSON 10.5

Matching: 1. b; 2. c; 3. d; 4. a

Word Math: The words are: necessary, secession, recession, recede, precede

LESSON 10.6

Guess the Meaning: Answers will vary. Check your class dictionary or an online dictionary of your preference for the exact meanings.

Web Quiz (Clockwise from top): omission, admit, intermittent, missile, transmission, emissary, permit

LESSON 10.7

Fill in the Blank: 1. fertile; 2. portfolio; 3. legislate; 4. defer

Web Quiz (Clockwise from top): import, collate, fertile, legislate, portable, correlate, aquifer

LESSON 10.8

Word Splits: 1. ap + peal; 2. re + pel + lent; 3. in + trud + e; 4. in + trus + ive; 5. com + puls + ion

What Doesn't Belong?: 1. repeal; 2. propeller; 3. push forward; 4. approve

LESSON 10.9

Matching: 1. d; 2. c; 3. a; 4. b

Pick the Word: 1. reject; 2. project; 3. object; 4. inject

LESSON 10.10

Change It Up: 1. rout; 2. bankrupt; 3. suffrage; 4. infraction

Web Quiz (Clockwise from top): infraction, routine, fragment, disrupt, fragile, abrupt, fracture or rupture

CHAPTER 10 REVIEW

Back "Words" Webs: Answers are listed by the "themes" for each web. Bend/Fold: reflex, deflect, replicate, reflect; Bring/Carry: defer, correlate, portable, import; Send: admit, permit, missile, emissary; Break/Shatter: fragile, bankrupt, disrupt, rout

REFERENCES

Farstrup, A. E., & Samuels, S. J. (Eds.). (2008). *What research has to say about vocabulary instruction*. Washington, D.C.: International Reading Association

Green, T. M. (1994). *The Greek and Latin roots of English*. Lanham, MD: Rowman and Littlefield.

Thompson, M. C. (2002). Vocabulary and grammar: Critical content for critical thinking. *The Journal of Secondary Gifted Education, 13*(2), 60–66.

ABOUT THE AUTHORS

Manisha Shelley Kaura is a high school senior from the Detroit area. It is her love for and curiosity of this beautiful English language that has carried her through this rather daunting project over the last 8 years. She is a Beatles maniac and loves Indian dance. In the fall of 2010, she will join a 6-year medical program specializing in pediatric neurology.

S. R. Kaura, M.D., is a family physician in private practice in the Detroit metro area. He is the author of two books on preventive medicine, *The Nibbler's Diet* and *Understanding and Preventing Cancer*. He has a special interest in historical linguistics.

Common Core State Standards Alignment

Grade Level	Common Core State Standards in ELA-Literacy
Grade 6	L.6.4 Determine or clarify the meaning of unknown and multiple-meaning words and phrases based on grade 6 reading and content, choosing flexibly from a range of strategies.
	L.6.5 Demonstrate understanding of figurative language, word relationships, and nuances in word meanings.
	L.6.6 Acquire and use accurately grade-appropriate general academic and domain-specific words and phrases; gather vocabulary knowledge when considering a word or phrase important to comprehension or expression.
Grade 7	L.7.4 Determine or clarify the meaning of unknown and multiple-meaning words and phrases based on grade 7 reading and content, choosing flexibly from a range of strategies.
	L.7.5 Demonstrate understanding of figurative language, word relationships, and nuances in word meanings.
	L.7.6 Acquire and use accurately grade-appropriate general academic and domain-specific words and phrases; gather vocabulary knowledge when considering a word or phrase important to comprehension or expression.
Grade 8	L.8.4 Determine or clarify the meaning of unknown and multiple-meaning words or phrases based on grade 8 reading and content, choosing flexibly from a range of strategies.
	L.8.5 Demonstrate understanding of figurative language, word relationships, and nuances in word meanings.
	L.8.6 Acquire and use accurately grade-appropriate general academic and domain-specific words and phrases; gather vocabulary knowledge when considering a word or phrase important to comprehension or expression.
Grade 9-10	L.9-10.4 Determine or clarify the meaning of unknown and multiple-meaning words and phrases based on grades 9–10 reading and content, choosing flexibly from a range of strategies.
	L.9-10.5 Demonstrate understanding of figurative language, word relationships, and nuances in word meanings.
	L.9-10.6 Acquire and use accurately general academic and domain-specific words and phrases, sufficient for reading, writing, speaking, and listening at the college and career readiness level; demonstrate independence in gathering vocabulary knowledge when considering a word or phrase important to comprehension or expression.

Printed in the United States
by Baker & Taylor Publisher Services